Martin de Porres
SAINT OF THE NEW WORLD

Martin

ILLUSTRATED BY JAMES FOX

LONDON: BURNS AND OATES

de Porres / *Saint*
of the New World

by Ellen Tarry

Vision Books

NEW YORK: FARRAR, STRAUS AND COMPANY

*This book is dedicated
to the hundreds of boys and girls,
young and old, who first heard
about Martin de Porres through my
teacher, Sister Mary Timothy, S.B.S.,
with the hope that we may all emulate
St. Martin's virtues of* CHARITY, JUSTICE
and LOVE *to the extent that we shall see a
brother in each man
whose hand we clasp and a sister
in each mother whose child we behold.*

Contents

Author's Note

It has been the great privilege of the author to know four of Martin de Porres' most effective American supporters: Rev. Thomas McGlynn, O.P., Rev. Norbert Georges, O.P., Sister Mary Timothy, S.B.S., and Eddie Doherty, the journalist.

In all of my literary efforts, with the exception of *The Third Door*, it has been possible to trace Sister Timothy's influence as the first point of interest, since she has been my teacher through the years. And so it goes that Sister Timothy was the first to tell me about the Mulatto of Lima, who had been declared Blessed.

At Friendship House in Harlem I met Eddie Doherty, and later Father Thomas McGlynn and Father Norbert Georges. Without these four, it is doubtful that my interest in Martin de Porres would have been sustained and that I would have had the patience to snatch stray minutes out of busy days to write this book. They will be surprised to know how they contributed to this story for, with the exception of Sister Timothy, our paths now seldom cross.

Though it was around 1936 that Sister Timothy first sent me a holy card bearing Martin de Porres' likeness, a renewed devotion to our saint had already begun to flower. From the sculptor-priest, Father McGlynn, I learned the part his statue of Martin played in this surge of love, prayer and homage.

In 1930, *The Colored Harvest*, a magazine of the Josephite Fathers, had published an article on Negro saints for Negro churches. Father McGlynn became interested in the idea and began some research. The one saintly man of color whose life intrigued him was, like himself, a Dominican. Perhaps the fact that Martin had overcome the handicap of being a half-breed to attain such an exalted position in seventeenth-century Peru, without relinquishing the humility which was at the core of his being, led this modern priest along the path which reached all the way to Rome and returned so recently in triumph. He gives credit for much of his interest in Martin to the biography by the English Jesuit, Rev. C. C. Martindale.

Father McGlynn finished his first statue of Martin in 1930, and that same year he was asked to show a piece of his work in an exhibit sponsored by the St. Hilda Art Guild, a group affiliated with the Episcopal Church. He chose the three-foot eight-inch plaster statue of Martin in his religious habit, a broom in his hand and mice at his feet. The statue attracted considerable attention from writers, artists and lecturers who saw the exhibit.

Years later, when the author worked at Friendship House in Chicago, Blessed Martin was the patron of our children's library. A friend sent us a small copy of the McGlynn statue, and I was surprised to learn that some people objected to this likeness of Martin. The broom seemed to them a symbol of servitude, rather than a reminder that Martin had used his broom to sweep away sin as well as dirt. A copy of this statue was presented to Pope John XXIII after St. Martin's canonization, and it is said to have been placed in the Pope's private apartment. Martin and his broom had traveled from a Protestant art exhibit in New York to a position of honor in the Vatican. This, to me, is a manifestation of the true spirit of brotherhood, which Martin de Porres espoused.

After the first novena in Blessed Martin's honor, which the Dominicans held at River Forest, Illinois, in 1935, articles on Martin began to appear in the Catholic press. Rev. Edward L. Hughes, O.P., who had founded the Blessed Martin Guild, contributed to various periodicals. Rev. J. C. Kearns wrote a book on Martin's life, and the Dominican magazine, *The Torch*, carried many articles about him. Yet no one wrote about Martin with more genuine affection than did Eddie Doherty. Eddie's hope was to one day cover the story of a genuine miracle which had resulted from prayers to Martin de Porres—and he never doubted that miracles would come as a result of Martin's intercession.

Father Norbert Georges, who succeeded Father Hughes at the Blessed Martin Guild, was kind enough to supply me with many of the pamphlets and books which have been written on the life of

Martin. One of the most helpful was *The Fifteenth Anniversary Book of The Blessed Martin Guild*, which consists of articles published in *The Torch* from 1935 to 1950, together with documents and transcripts of the testimony of witnesses to miracles performed by Blessed Martin during his lifetime. Father Kearns's book supplied the facts on which this book is based, except for the time Martin spent in Quayaquil with his father's uncle. That chapter, as well as most of the dialogue throughout the book, is largely the result of poetic license. Only a few of the many miracles attributed to Martin de Porres have been mentioned in this book.

I could not conclude this note without acknowledging the encouragement I have received from my friend, George K. Hunton, of the Catholic Interracial Council; the constructive criticism of my daughter, Elizabeth Tarry Patton; the prayers of the Dominican Sisters at Mount St. Mary in Newburgh, N.Y.; and the patient guidance of my editor, Clare Costello, who waited four years for this manuscript.

CHAPTER *1*

Martin and Juana

The little girl stood in front of a shabby adobe house on the street called Espíritu Santo and begged to go with her brother.

"Why *can't* I go to the market place with you?" Juana asked again.

"Because you're not old enough and your legs are not long enough," Martin de Porres told his sister.

"I'm six years old and you are only eight," Juana declared.

"But you're a girl," Martin said, only because he could think of no other excuse. "And, besides, Mama told me to take care of you. The trip to the market place is a long one. If you dust the house for me while I am away, I'll bring you the sweetest mango in the whole square."

Juana's face brightened at the mention of her favorite fruit. Martin knew he had won. She is so sweet, he thought, I hate to say unkind things and make her sad, but it would never do for her to go to the market place with me. She might say one word that would give everything away. Then Mama would be more cross than ever.

Martin lost no time. Soon he was skipping along over the cobblestones of Espíritu Santo, which was little more than a narrow opening in the poorest section of Lima, Peru.

Mornings in Lima were nearly always chilly and damp, but Martin paid no attention to the weather. He waved cheerfully to the neighbors and did not dream that as they watched him skipping down the street they shook their heads and whispered. It was sad to see a child out on so damp a morning without a cloak about his shoulders or sandals on his feet because his mother was too poor to buy them.

Martin looked at the empty basket on his arm and wondered how much he would get for the coins he clutched in his right hand. He must get twice as much as anyone else. That would mean going from stall to stall, begging, bluffing and bargaining with the merchants. This always took time.

If Juana will dust for me, Martin thought, the house will be in order. Then I shall save the best of everything for our table and that will make Mama happy. I hope the others will be happy too. A frown crossed Martin's brow when he thought of the beggars who waited for him in the market place. He wished he had twice as much money because it seemed that each day he had to feed twice as many as the day before.

The boy's brown legs stretched and his pace quickened. In a little while the poverty of Espíritu Santo was behind him and he was trotting through a more fashionable section of Lima. The heavy morning fog began to lift and Martin was aware of the large houses with patios and flower gardens on either side of the street. Through the open windows he glimpsed servants, and there were gardeners tending the flowers. He thought about the boys and girls who lived in these houses. Where were they, he wondered, and what did they do all day? The boy smiled as he remembered that few households in Lima arose as early as his.

The two-storied Spanish houses, their flower gardens splashed with brilliant colors, reminded Martin of a picture he had found in an old chest. His mother had said it came from Spain and that it was a sketch of the street on which his father, Don Juan de Porres, had been born. Martin remembered the harsh scolding his mother had given him one day when she found him daydreaming over the picture instead of doing the housework. She did not want to be reminded of his father, who had deserted the family when Juana was a baby.

Martin's pace slackened as he walked along. Suddenly he heard his name called and looked up to find himself in front of the Church of San Sebastian, where he had been christened on November 9, 1579, the day of his birth. The priest who stood calling on the steep steps was dwarfed by the shadow of the church's façade and lofty towers.

"Martin," Father Antonio said, laughing, "you slip away from the church each morning before I can speak with you. I have been hearing things at the market place. The merchants tell me you are one of their regular customers. I did not know that your mother was so wealthy."

"Padre, the merchants are very kind to me," Martin explained as a flush spread over his copper-colored face. "They give me much more than I deserve in return for the few coins my mother can spare."

Martin bowed respectfully and hurried away before Father Antonio could ask more questions.

During the two years since Ana had first taken her son to the market place where the merchants kept their stalls, Martin had learned a great deal about bargaining and about the beggars who gathered there in the hope of getting a crust of bread or a piece of fruit. Twice Ana had whipped her son for giving them food he had bought for the family. The last time, Martin had promised his mother that he would never give her food away again. Now he earned a coin or two by doing errands for the neighbors or delivering a package for a merchant—and he had learned to buy where he could get the most for the smallest amount.

As Martin approached the square he saw many of his beggar friends waiting. The money he had earned was safe in his pocket. He decided he would show only the coins his mother had given him. He would produce *his* money only if and when efforts to bargain failed.

The cries of the beggars soon mingled with the raucous laughter of soldiers and sailors, the shrill bargaining of the merchants, and the prancing feet of the grandees' fine horses who were likely to ride down any who did not get out of their way.

Martin could not understand how the rich men he saw in suits of broadcloth, silk and satin, wearing slippers with buckles that looked like silver, and big hats with plumes, could pass the half-naked beggars as if they did not hear their piteous pleas or see their outstretched hands.

Nevertheless Martin was fascinated by the airs of the Spanish grandees. He always wondered if his father looked like these men. But today Martin could not stop to daydream about Don Juan. People were rushing from stall to stall. Beggars, children and dogs were cluttering up the walk, and Martin had to get on with his shopping.

He walked back and forth, compared prices, begged a little here and made a good bargain there, and soon he had filled his basket with fruits, vegetables and bread. The food for his mother was tucked away safely in one part of the basket, with Juana's mango. The extra food he would give away. Moreover, he still had one coin in his pocket. Martin felt rather proud of his accomplishments until he began to distribute the food: a handful of raisins to one beggar, a piece of bread to another, fruit to a father with a sickly child, vegetables to an old man who said he wanted to make a broth for his ailing wife.

Martin had reached the last stall in the square when he came upon a Portuguese woman he had never seen before. Three half-naked children huddled near her. Their stomachs protruded, and one could almost count their ribs. The mother held out her hand to Martin without saying a word. The plea in her eyes touched the boy's heart and it was only a matter of moments before he had given her all that was left in the basket—Juana's mango included.

As Martin walked away from the woman, he felt the one coin tucked away in a pocket of his breeches. Now I am really in trouble, he thought. I cannot go home with an empty basket. He began to walk from one stall to another, trying to decide where to make a bold effort to buy bread and vegetables with what he had. A ship had docked early in the morning, and now the sailors were filling the square, keeping the storekeepers busy. Suddenly Martin remembered Old Tomás. Tomás was a friend of Martin's father; perhaps he would help him. The old man had told Martin many things about Don Juan: he was a Knight of Alcantara, a soldier to King Philip II, and had once served in Panama. Now Don Juan represented the king in Ecuador.

Martin headed for Old Tomás's stall. The beggars appeared surprised to see their young friend retracing his steps. Some tried to stop him, but Martin shook them off and broke into a trot. He outran every beggar he saw, stopping for nothing until he reached Tomás's stall.

The elderly merchant was standing in front, wringing his hands as he looked up and down the square. His face lighted up when he saw the boy. "I thought you would never come," he said.

"I have only this," Martin panted, taking the single coin from his pocket, "and I must get food for my mother and a mango for my little sister. I know what you are thinking, but if you will only help me this time I will promise never to give the food away again."

The old man laughed as Martin had never

heard him laugh before. "All you think about is food, food, food." The man threw up his hands in mock desperation. "You feed every beggar in the square, and yet when I send them to look for you not a one can find you."

"Send for me?" Martin asked. "Why would you send for me?"

The boy looked from the group of beggars who had gathered in front of the stall back to the merchant, whose faded blue eyes seemed to be almost dancing.

"A ship docked in the harbor this morning," began Tomás. "Where do you think she sailed from, and who do you think was on board?"

"I guess the *sailors* were on board," replied Martin, still puzzled but now beginning to look over Tomás's stock, mentally picking out the vegetables and fruit he would try to buy with his coin.

"The sailors!" Old Tomás laughed. "Would I be sending for you just because another boat-load of sailors landed in Lima? Don Juan de Porres was on that boat!"

"Tomás! Do you mean it?" Martin almost dropped his empty basket. "Don Juan—my father—is really in Lima *now?*"

"Here's the proof." The old man produced a sheet of paper covered with a fine script.

"He sent me this note as soon as they dropped anchor. Here's his name—Don Juan de Porres—right here."

Martin was too excited to read the signature. "There's nothing in the house," he whispered. "Not a bite of bread or a piece of fruit, and it's all my fault."

Tomás smothered his impulse to laugh at the boy's woeful expression. He knew that Martin was no ordinary lad and therefore not to be laughed at. Only a week before, Tomás had watched Martin double his fist and bite a lip rather than fight a boy who had taunted him because he was a half-breed. Quietly, the man picked up the basket Martin had dropped and began filling it with food.

"This is all I have." Martin offered the coin. "Would you give me bread for my mother and one ripe mango for Juana?"

"There is no need for me to remind you" —Old Tomás pinched Martin's cheek—"that you had no right to give your mother's food to the beggars. You may keep that coin, and there will be more than enough food in your basket. Go straight home and tell your mother. If I know your father, he will not go any-where until his tailor and barber have finished with him. So be on your way." Old Tomás gave Martin a push as he handed him the basket filled with the best his shelves had to offer.

The beggars outside the stall had heard snatches of the conversation. They agreed among themselves that nobody was to ask Martin to share the food Old Tomás had given him.

"What's wrong with you now?" Tomás asked, when the boy made no attempt to leave the stall.

"How—how do you know my father will want to see me—or my sister?" Martin asked, remembering that once when his mother had been angry, she had said that his Spanish father had deserted her because her children's skin was dark.

This time Old Tomás threw his hands up in real desperation. "First it was food and now it's questions," he sighed. "Well—if you must know, a missionary from one of our convents visited Ecuador. He told your father about you and how helpful you had been to the Dominicans, and your father said he wanted to see you. Why would I be wasting time looking for you if your father had not told me? Be off, silly boy!"

Martin gave one big leap and was out of the stall. Old Tomás and the beggars laughed to see him run so fast that he dropped a bunch of vegetables and a piece of fruit without being aware of his loss. The beggars ran behind him, pushing and shoving each other to grab what had fallen from the basket. The tallest in the crowd was also the fastest, and he held his prize high, out of the reach of the others, so that Old Tomás saw what it was.

The merchant sighed as he went back to his stall. "There are more vegetables," he recalled, "but it is lucky I put two mangos in the basket, for it *would* be a mango that poor Martin dropped. He's so excited he'll never know the difference, and his friends got a tidbit after all."

While Tomás was chuckling over Martin, the boy was running so fast that his breath cut his chest like pinpricks. When he reached Espíritu Santo the neighbors came out of their adobes to see who was chasing him. They called to ask what was wrong, but Martin paid no attention. His only thought was to get home. Reaching the door of the house, the boy remembered his promise to Juana and looked in the basket for the mango. His heart sank, for he recalled seeing the ripe yellow-red fruit on top of the basket. Quickly he pushed aside lemons, avocados, dates and a custard-apple until he found the other mango Old Tomás had sent.

I will give her the fruit first, he thought, and then I will tell her.

As Martin opened the door, Juana heard him. "Where is it? Did you get it, Martin?" she called as she ran to her brother.

"Get what?" Martin held the fruit behind him.

"My mango!" the little girl insisted. "You promised!"

"All this excitement—and still you cry for fruit, like a baby."

"What excitement?" Juana asked as she snatched the mango from her brother.

"You and your mango!" Martin frowned. "You almost made me forget. Our father is here, Juana. He's here in Lima and he is coming to see us!"

"Our father?" Juana had no memory of a father. "Do you mean we will have a mother *and* a father?"

"Yes, but you must wash your face and comb your hair," the boy said. "I guess you'll have to put on the dress you wear to church."

In their haste the children forgot that they had not finished setting the house in order. They were so engrossed in trying to make

Juana presentable that neither of them heard
the tall, dark woman enter the room. She
would have been beautiful if bitterness and
worry had not etched deep lines in her face.
Before the children were even aware of her
presence, her hand was raised as if to strike
Martin.

"I told you," she shouted, "to have this
house cleaned before I came back."

"Our father—Don Juan de Porres—was on
the boat that docked this morning!" the boy
cried, and his mother drew back, startled.
"He's coming here to see us. Old Tomás told
me."

Ana Velasquez looked at her son in astonishment. "Old Tomás said Don Juan is coming
here?" she asked, sinking into a chair near the
table. "You're sure he's coming here?"

Martin felt sorry for Ana when he saw her
put her head on the table and weep. He motioned for Juana to join him and the children
each put an arm about their mother to console
her. "We don't have much time," Martin
whispered. "Old Tomás said Don Juan would
see his barber and the tailor before he came to
us. The house has been swept and dusted
and . . ."

Ana raised her head and looked at both of

her children as if she had never seen them before. How unfair, she thought. I am filled with bitterness and ill will, and it is my children who suffer. She pulled them to her in a hug.

"Perhaps," Martin told their mother after they had put on the only decent clothes they owned, "our father will decide that we are clean and neat, even if our skin is not so fair as his and our hair is not straight."

At that very moment Don Juan was chuckling over Old Tomás's story of Martin and the mango. The knight had been pleased with his friend's account of the boy's shrewdness in dealing with the merchants—but he was slightly puzzled when Old Tomás told him that Martin was often at prayer during the day. Neither could he understand why Martin took on the responsibility of feeding the beggars.

"Nobody would expect my son to be so pious," Don Juan said, laughing.

"Already they say the little girl is a beauty," Tomás went on. "She reminds me of her mother when she first came from Panama. And I seem to remember the time when her father was considered one of the most handsome knights in His Majesty's service."

Don Juan's proud heart was touched. "Get

me a horse," he called to his servant. "I must
go to see my children at once," he told Tomás.

News of Don Juan's arrival had spread
through Lima. Ana's neighbors went from
house to house to pass the word along, though
none of them dared approach her little adobe.
They knew that Ana never spoke of her children's father and rewarded with the darkest of
looks any who mentioned his name.

The people who lived on Espíritu Santo
were an odd assortment. Most of them were
half-breeds like Martin and Juana, a few were
Negroes like Ana, and there were several Indians. One or two families were Portuguese or
Spanish.

Within an hour, the clop-clop of Don Juan's
fine white horse's hoofs sounded the alarm, and
the neighbors ran out of their houses. Martin,
who had been watching from the doorway,
told his mother what was happening. An old
man held Don Juan's horse while the nobleman
alighted. The women bowed and some of them
held up children who, they explained, had been
born since he went away. Don Juan passed
out pieces of gold to those he remembered best.

When Ana and the children appeared in the
doorway, the neighbors became silent. Martin,

usually so resourceful, could not think of a thing to do or say. His mother, he decided, might well have been a statue, so motionless was she as she stood looking at Don Juan with the neighbors all around him.

It was little Juana who broke the awkwardness. When she smiled at her father and curtsied sweetly, the neighbors seemed relieved, too. They cried, "Bravo! Bravo!" as Don Juan held out his arms to his children.

Ana still did not move. After Don Juan had embraced the children, he raised his head and his eyes met Ana's. Without saying a word, she turned and walked back into the house, her little family following.

Though the house was clean, Don Juan was struck by its bareness. He realized that he had neglected his children, and the thought made him uncomfortable and silent. Ana gave him no help, but Martin offered his father one of the two chairs. Then Juana sat on her father's knee, as she had seen other children do, and patted his face.

"Ana," Don Juan began, "this is a pretty child. And I hear that the boy shows signs of excellent character."

"I have been able to give them very little,"

Ana replied in a strained voice, "but I have done the best I could."

"I am sorry that I have been away so long," was the way Don Juan apologized for his neglect. "Please sit down. We must talk."

For a moment, Martin thought that his mother was going to continue to be unfriendly to Don Juan. He pushed the chair in her direction, giving her no excuse to remain standing. Though Ana accepted the chair, she said nothing. As Martin wondered what else he could do, he spied the cavalier's hat, which his father had placed on the table. Then Martin eased around to that side of the table, pushed the hat in the line of Juana's vision, and waited hopefully.

In a few seconds Martin was rewarded.

"Your hat is pretty." Juana reached for it. "Your suit is pretty, too, and your shoes are shiny. I Like you!" she told her father.

Don Juan laughed. "And you are pretty, too," he said and kissed the little girl's forehead.

Martin watched happily. Obviously the situation had eased. Now was the time to run to church for a quick visit of thanksgiving. As he trotted along, Martin kept wondering about his father's words a moment before. "It is time Juana came to know her father," Don Juan had said, "and time for her father to make plans for Juana and her brother. That is one of the reasons I am in Lima."

When Martin returned from church, Juana was playing in front of the house. Inside he found his father still talking with his mother.

"I will admit I had only intended to *see* the children and leave money with you for them," Don Juan was saying. "But these are no ordinary children. The girl is like a delicate flower, and Martin"—Don Juan smiled as the boy entered the room—"does the family name proud."

"I am glad you are pleased," Ana said without smiling.

"It is more than that," Don Juan continued. "I must prepare for their future. The missionaries have told me, Old Tomás has told me, and now my heart tells me. Martin must have a proper education and there are no free schools in Lima, even if our university is the first one established in the New World. As for Juana—you cannot train her, Ana, according to the social standards of a Spanish family of noble descent. This you must admit."

Martin became uneasy. He saw a strange expression in his mother's eyes. He was not sure what his father was talking about, but he did not have long to wait.

"These children must be educated." Don Juan placed his hand firmly on the rickety table beside him. "I must take them with me to Quayaquil, where they can live in the home of my uncle, Don Diego de Miranda. There they will be tutored and trained as befits the children of a noble Spanish family."

Martin was not sure why he called to his sister to come in from her play. He just felt that his mother needed them. The slow smile which changed Ana's face when she saw the two children, was all the reward the boy wanted.

"I will ask the children what they want to do," she managed to say.

"You must understand," Don Juan continued, "that though I came here to see the governor on behalf of His Majesty, I sought this assignment so as to have the opportunity to see the children. I will be here only a few days. We must decide this matter at once."

"I will ask the children," Ana repeated. "Martin, Juana, do you want to go to Ecuador with your father? He can give you a good home. You will learn to read and write and count numbers. And you will never have to be a servant—like your mother."

Martin knew that his mother was far from happy. Yet it had all happened so quickly that neither child could find words.

"They are both good children," Ana continued. She turned to Don Juan. "I am grateful to you for giving them this opportunity."

Quickly it was settled. Martin and Juana would sail to Ecuador with Don Juan. He would let Ana know when the boat would leave. Meanwhile she would buy clothes for the children with the money he gave her.

After Don Juan had mounted his horse and rode away, the neighbors came to see what he had brought. Juana lost no time in telling them that her father was taking Martin and her away on a big ship. Ana spoke as one in a trance when she told her friends of Don Juan's proposal. They made her repeat it again and again, and even then they could hardly believe. To them, this meant that the Holy Spirit had finally smiled on the street called Espíritu Santo.

One day, as Martin listened to the endless chatter of the women who had come to join in the excitement, he felt a strong urge to

chase them all away and tell his mother that
he was not going to leave her. He had not
been fooled by Ana's sharp words at the end
of a long day or even by the whippings she
had given him. He knew that she loved him
and he wondered what her life would be like
after he and Juana went with his father.
Martin was troubled, and there was only one
place for him to go. Sadly he made his way
to church.

When Martin left church he turned toward
the market place. Old Tomás had been sending food to the family since Don Juan's
return, so Martin had been unable to visit his
friends, the beggars. Now he went directly to
the stall of Tomás, from whom he extracted a
promise to set aside one basket of food each
day for the beggars.

No doubt the fruit would be over-ripe and
the bread slightly stale and the vegetables in
danger of wilting thought Martin on the way
home, but that will be better than nothing. I
must trust God to look after them and my
poor Mama, who will be all alone until I can
come back to them.

CHAPTER 2

Off to Ecuador

The day finally came when Martin and Juana were to sail away to Ecuador. Don Juan arrived at Ana Velasquez's in a fine carriage, and the neighbors crowded into Ana's house to tell Martin and Juana good-by. The children waved as the carriage rolled away. Shouts of "*Adios! Adios!*" could be heard long after Espíritu Santo was out of sight.

Don Juan was pleased to see how happy Juana was as they rode toward the harbor. Martin's apparent sadness was therefore all the more puzzling to his father. The boy felt Don Juan's gaze searching his face, but how could he say that he was sad because he had seen tears in his mother's eyes as they rode away?

The sight of the beggars in the market place, their outstretched hands unnoticed by the soldiers and sailors who crowded in and out of the stalls, was more than Martin could bear. A rebellious sob escaped and Don Juan saw that tears streamed down his son's cheeks.

"Only women weep." Don Juan did not attempt to hide his annoyance. "The son of Don Juan de Porres is not expected to act like a woman. Why are you not happy like your sister?"

"Oh, *padre mio*"—Martin addressed Don Juan as Father for the first time—"the poor are so hungry. See, some of them are half-naked. And we—we have so much!" The boy looked at his father hopefully.

Don Juan ordered the driver to halt. Then he told him to walk the horse until they were past the square. Don Juan would not let this boy, the son of a Negro mother, put a knight of Alcantara to shame. He took a handful of coins from his pouch and threw them to Martin's beggars, who seemed to appear as if by magic all along the way to the wharf.

By the time they glimpsed the Spanish ships riding at anchor on the bay with the royal pennant of King Philip II fluttering from each masthead, Martin's sadness had vanished. The proud galleons looked like highly polished wooden houses with sails attached. Neither of the children had ever seen anything like this before, and they made no attempt to hide their awe.

Spanish soldiers stood about the wharf in little groups. Martin had not realized what an important man his father was until he saw the soldiers salute and make way for the carriage when Don Juan leaned out of the window.

"They are some of the bravest men you will ever see," Martin's father explained, as he led the children to the ship which was to take them to Ecuador. "They are carrying the Spanish flag all over the world."

While Don Juan was giving orders to his servants, who were storing the many boxes he was taking back to Quayaquil, Martin and Juana stood along the deck of the vessel and watched the men who were loading the cargo.

Though some of the laborers were Spanish, Portuguese and Indian, Martin noticed that most of them were Negro slaves. To Juana it was all a part of a wonderful sight, but each time Martin saw a black man stagger beneath the weight of a heavy load the boy felt as if the weight was on his own shoulders.

When Don Juan joined the children, Martin asked his father what was in the huge crates and bags he saw the slaves put aboard the ship. Don Juan explained that the men were loading gold which had been taken from the mines of Peru.

"Where is it going?" Martin wanted to know.

"Eventually to Spain," his father replied.

"Does the gold from Peru belong to Spain?" the boy asked.

"In a few weeks," the proud man laughed, "your tutor will tell you that all Peru and most of the New World belongs to Spain. Martin, you ask such serious questions for a boy of your age. Look at Juana. Her eyes are like dancing fireflies on a dark night. In an hour's time we will be under way." He smiled. "Then I shall see what kind of sailors you are."

Martin could see people on the wharf pointing up at them. He wondered if they were saying: "Look, that's Don Juan de Porres. He's taking Ana Velasquez's children back to Ecuador with him."

Suddenly the boat shuddered. Martin held on to the rail and Don Juan took Juana in his arms.

"It's moving!" the boy cried. "The wharf is moving!"

"The ship is moving." Don Juan smiled, as he held Juana high so that she might have a better view. "And it is carrying you out to sea."

Martin gave no sign of having heard his father, for he had seen a familiar figure on the wharf. It was the figure of a woman—a tall, dark woman—with a shawl on her head that fell about her shoulders. She was standing apart from the crowd. The boy shaded his eyes to make sure. Yes, he thought, it is my mother, and she would not come to the boat because my father did not ask her.

Then Martin saw another familiar figure: an old Indian who begged outside a fruit stall where Martin traded. This old man was one of the few beggars who had not been in the public square when Don Juan's carriage drove past. Even then he had been hobbling in the

direction of the wharf so that he might take
leave of the boy who was his only true friend.
As the wind filled the sails, the wharf seemed
farther away, but not so far that Martin could
not see Ana bow her head.

"*Madre mia, madre mia,*" the boy called in
clear tones which he hoped would travel
across the water between them. "I'll come
back—I'll come back—"

Startled by Martin's cries, Don Juan followed the boy's gaze and recognized the
shawled figure on the receding shore. Always
the knight, he set Juana down so that her
happy excitement would not be marred by
another leave-taking, then raised his hat and
bowed to the woman who had mothered his
children.

Martin and Juana surprised their father.
They proved to have exceptionally sturdy sea
legs and Don Juan grew more proud of them
each day. They were the only children aboard
ship, and while the captain showed them certain attentions because of their father's position,
the passengers and the sailors became attached
to them because of their gentle manners.

Martin and Juana had never been outside of
Lima before, and the trip was a time of
wonder for them. They laughed when the ship

rolled with the waves and Juana clapped her hands in delight when the rays of sunlight danced on the water like brilliant needles. Don Juan complained because the food, after the first few days, consisted largely of biscuits and wine. But Martin and Juana ate the hard bread as if it had been cake. Martin loved best the evenings aboard ship, when the sailors sang hymns to Our Lady.

Each day they sailed closer and closer to Quayaquil, where Don Juan's uncle, Don Diego, would meet the ship and learn for the first time of the existence of his nephew's children.

While the sailors and wharf-hands struggled to dock the ship at Quayaquil, Martin looked solemnly toward the wharf where a handsome gray-haired gentleman stood waving. This was Don Diego.

Then the gangplank was in place and Don Juan and his uncle were embracing. Martin and Juana stood together as their father explained to his uncle that they were his children. Martin watched the old man struggle to conceal his surprise, and the boy had the feeling that his father's uncle was trying to decide what to do with two half-breed children.

Startled as he was, Don Diego was quick to see that Martin and Juana were exhausted from the long voyage and the excitement. It was clear that he must first see to food and rest for the children. Doña Lucita, the elderly cousin who had acted as his housekeeper since his wife's death, would have to be notified that they were coming. Decisions about the future could wait until tomorrow.

Don Diego sent his message and returned to find Martin and Juana huddled in a dark corner of the deck while their father shouted orders to the sailors in the hold and rushed about, seeing to the king's cargo for which he was responsible. Don Diego took one look at them—little Juana's sleepy head resting on her brother's shoulder, while he seemed to be having a hard time keeping his own eyes open—and hurried off to berate his startled nephew angrily. "What can you be thinking of? Look at those poor children—and you are concerned only with your own business! I shall take them home and see that they are fed and put to bed." Then he added coldly, "The carriage will return for you later—if you wish to join us."

Don Juan was even more surprised to see the tenderness with which his uncle took Juana in his arms and carried her from the boat to the carriage, as Martin followed wearily behind.

The carriage sped through the streets of Quayaquil so fast that Martin thought the houses, the streets, and the palm trees were sailing past them. Don Diego smiled at the boy's obvious bewilderment and patted his hand in assurance, while the old man tightened his hold on the sleeping child for fear the swaying motion of the carriage would awaken her.

The horses had left the main road and turned onto a winding driveway which was lined with cocoanut palm trees when Martin felt a jolt as Juana sat upright in Don Diego's arms. "Where am I?" the little girl cried. "Where is my father? I want my brother!"

"Your father will be with you very soon." Don Diego spoke softly. "And here is your brother who takes such excellent care of you, and there"—he pointed to a great house in the distance—"is your new home."

Martin held out his hand to Juana, but already she was peering out the window of the carriage, the better to see where she was going to live. He could not blame her for being curious because it did not seem possible that they could be taken from the little adobe

on Espíritu Santo to the huge house to which
they were drawing closer.

"We will live there?" Juana asked.

"Yes." Don Diego and Martin exchanged
knowing smiles about Juana's curiosity.

"It's like the houses where the rich people
live in Lima," Martin thought, remembering
the many times he had wondered about the
children who lived in the big houses. "But it
doesn't seem fair for us to live like this while
Mama is still on Espíritu Santo and many of
my friends in the market place have nowhere
to sleep."

The carriage came to a halt before an iron
gate. The gate was opened, and soon the carriage had stopped again before Don Diego's
beautiful home. Martin and Juana followed
Don Diego inside. Never before, except in
the cathedral, had the boy seen so many
beautiful paintings or so many fine furnishings.
He could feel Juana trembling as she clutched
his hand.

Doña Lucita met them in the great hall.

"These are the children—Don Juan's children," Don Diego told her. "Martin, Juana,
this is Doña Lucita."

Martin thought Doña Lucita's eyes were as
black as the black taffeta dress she was wearing.

He could not remember ever having seen anyone with skin so fair. Her back was straight as an arrow, and at first she seemed stern, but then she smiled warmly. "Welcome to Quayaquil." Doña Lucita extended a hand to each child, and Martin was glad his mother had taught Juana how to curtsy. "I know you must be tired after such a journey," she continued. "Come with me."

Martin and Juana slept soundly and gratefully in their massive beds, each in a beautifully furnished room. They were too tired even to be lonely for each other or for Mama.

While the children slept, Don Juan sat with his uncle and Doña Lucita, telling them about Ana and the many ways in which he had neglected his children. They all agreed that past mistakes might well be forgot and every effort made to educate Martin and his sister.

"There is something about the boy that puzzles me," Don Juan said. "But the girl"—he chuckled—"she's a pretty little imp. I think I understand her."

Martin and Juana soon learned that their father, as well as his uncle, was an important man in Quayaquil. Doña Lucita and the nurse, Anita, looked after Juana, but Martin became a "second son" to Don Diego. There was

room in the older man's saddle for a slight
boy like Martin, and many of his waking
hours were spent riding over the vast plantation which was covered with squatty little
trees or bushes from which the many laborers
who worked for Don Diego picked dark
berries that would be husked, roasted and
ground to make cocoa.

There were no public schools in Quayaquil,
and the elderly Spanish scholar who tutored
the children of many of the best families was
summoned to Don Diego's home to begin the
education of Martin and his sister. Both children were taught the alphabet and learned to
read and write their names. They learned to
count, though Juana soon tired of numbers,
and the indulgent Anita often rescued the little
girl from her demanding teacher. It was clear
that Juana was the pet of the household.

Martin and Juana were taught when to
stand, when to sit, and how to speak in the
presence of their elders, how to bow with ease
and grace when being presented, even how to
pray at set and proper times.

Quayaquil soon began to seem like home to
the children. Don Diego did his best to make
them happy, even to arranging for a daily
Mass in the chapel by the gate because Martin

longed to go to Mass each morning as he had done in Lima. After a time he was allowed to go with an elderly servant to distribute food to the poor, and then his happiness knew no bounds.

Martin enjoyed the hours he spent with his tutor, who told Don Juan that it had been years since he had found so apt a pupil. Already the boy was exploring the joys of reading, and once or twice each week Don Juan sat with his son while the boy read aloud from one of the books on the table in the room which had once been his father's.

Martin and Juana had made their home with their father's family for two years when the next big change took place. Martin and Don Diego were about to ride out to the fields. A servant was holding the horse, and Juana and Doña Lucita stood watching them as they prepared to mount. Then Don Juan's horse approached the gate, and it was evident that Martin's father was disturbed. He barely spoke to the children, but he told his uncle he wanted to see him at once. Then he handed the reins of his horse to the servant and rushed into the house. Doña Lucita was as dumbfounded as the children. In a few moments, however, she too went into the house and left them alone. Juana, who was not accustomed to being ignored, started to whimper, but Martin could only stand and wonder.

In a few moments Doña Lucita returned and told the children they were to follow her. She led them to the library where they found their father and Don Diego examining a document Don Juan held in his hand. Martin and Juana stood respectfully and waited, as they had been taught to do in the presence of their elders.

Don Diego cleared his throat. "A great honor has come to your father," he said. "The king of Spain has appointed him governor of Panama. Only men who have shown exceptional diplomatic skill, daring, courage and intelligence are chosen to govern in the New World. Martin, I am sure you understand that it is from these possessions that we get the gold and silver which bolsters the power of our great country," and the old man waved his hands as if a rich and powerful Spain lay just outside his window.

Juana tugged at Martin's shirt sleeve, and he knew she was trying to tell him that she did not understand what Don Diego was talking about. Martin was not sure that he himself understood.

Don Diego continued, "I have asked your father to let you children stay here at Quayaquil. Though you appear robust enough, we have lost hundreds of men from the malaria which breeds in swamplands such as are found in Panama. We would not think of letting you risk that danger!"

Doña Lucita put an arm about Juana. "What Don Diego means is that we do not want you and Martin to leave us just because your father is going away. Don Diego says it's because of the malaria in Panama, but—"

"Where is my father going? I don't want him to go away!" Juana burst into tears.

While the men looked helpless, Doña Lucita tried to explain to the child that her father had to go to Panama because the king had ordered him to do so. When she finally understood, Juana cried louder than ever. Doña Lucita took her away, but her sobs could be heard even after they had left the room.

Don Diego and Martin's father kept looking at the boy, and he knew he must say something. Though he had been happy in Quayaquil, he could not help feeling guilty about the many comforts he had enjoyed. It had always seemed quite like a dream. Now that the dream was ending, he was almost glad.

Don Juan sat with head bowed. He had been touched by Juana's grief. Now he had to steel himself for the separation from the son who had confided to him only a few days before that he hoped to study medicine one day. What a joy it would have been to watch him grow, the father thought.

"Well?" Don Diego broke the silence. "Martin, will you stay with us?"

"I will do what my father wishes me to do," Martin said quietly, "but I know I am needed in Lima. I want to take care of my mother and help the beggars who depended on me."

"What about your sister?" Don Diego asked.

"Juana belongs here and she will stay. I shall hate to leave you and Doña Lucita, but I should like to return to Lima—if my father will not object."

"Final decisions must wait until tomorrow." Don Juan's voice belied his unruffled countenance, and Martin knew that his father's heart was heavy.

The next day Don Diego talked with Martin for almost an hour, trying to persuade him to stay in Quayaquil. Juana, too, begged her brother not to leave her, but it was finally agreed that Don Juan would take the boy back to Lima, and then go on to his post in Panama.

Martin was only eleven years old, but as he began preparations for the second voyage with his father he felt like a man of the world. When he thought of being separated from Juana for the first time in their lives, he would push the image of her tear-stained face away and think of how happy his mother would look when he returned to her. Each time he thought of leaving the little chapel by the gate, he sought out the old servant who had promised to serve the Padre's Mass and made him renew his promise.

The day Martin left Don Diego's house, the old man was prouder of the boy than he had ever been. Martin and his father sat in one carriage, piled high with Don Juan's belongings and the boy's few possesions, including the books which had been the father's. Juana rode to the wharf in another carriage, with Doña Lucita and Don Diego. All of the house servants and most of the workers from the fields crowded around Martin to tell him good-by. Don Diego pretended to be impatient, but when Anita began to cry, the old uncle was afraid that Juana too would soon be weeping. He ordered all of the servants to return to their work.

Martin blessed himself as the carriage passed

the little chapel, and could not help but remember how forlorn he had felt that first day
in Quayaquil. Then Don Juan began to talk
about the surgeon to whom Martin would be
apprenticed in Lima, and by the time they
reached the wharf and Don Juan pointed out
their boat, Martin felt a tinge of the same excitement he had known the first day of that
other voyage.

Doña Lucita and Don Diego insisted on
boarding the boat to make sure that Martin
had comfortable quarters. Then it was Don
Juan's turn to remember the fears he had
known the day he first presented his children
to his uncle.

Juana kept saying that she did not want to
go back to Lima. Yet when it was time to go
ashore and leave Martin and her father, she
tried to make them leave the boat with her.
Doña Lucita and Don Diego had to promise
the little girl everything they could remember
she had ever asked for in order to get her to
say good-by and walk down the gangplank
with them. Martin could not help wondering
if he would ever see his sister again.

CHAPTER 3

Lima Again

Martin stood on the deck of the ship which was to take him back to Lima and waved to his sister. He could see that she was crying, but Don Diego had a protective arm about her, and Martin knew that the uncle would take good care of her. Don Juan had left money with his uncle for Juana's support, and there was a sum set aside to be used as a dowry, in case Don Juan did not return before she reached the age of marriage.

The sadness of parting with Juana and the rest of the family was pushed aside by the pleasure Martin found in the close companionship with his father. As the days passed it was evident that Don Juan was genuinely concerned over the boy's future, even though he was often astounded by the mature reasoning Martin displayed. One of their favorite topics was the matter of a proper education. As the journey neared its end, Don Juan pressed himself and the boy for final decisions.

"Before I leave Lima," Martin's father said, "I must make sure that you have been confirmed. Then we must make plans for your training. I want you to be prepared to make a comfortable living. We do not know what awaits me in Panama. Are you sure you want to become a surgeon?"

"Oh, yes, Padre," Martin answered with enthusiasm.

"That will require much study," Don Juan reminded him.

"I know," Martin replied with a smile. "But when I have finished I can heal the poor as well as feed them."

Don Juan studied the face of his son before

he spoke. "I am not sure that I understand your compulsion to care for the poor," he admitted. "But perhaps it is neither intended nor necessary that I understand. I am convinced you are a good boy, though a bit—a bit unusual for your age. However, as the son of Don Juan de Porres, you deserve the best education possible. I will make arrangements for you to be apprenticed to my friend Marcelo de Rivero, the most skilled barber-surgeon in all Peru."

When the ship docked at Lima, Martin was trembling with excitement. He had looked forward to rushing to the market place as soon as he left the boat to see if any of his old friends were there. To his dismay, a carriage stood on the wharf. In a moment he was hustled into it, and the horses were racing through the familiar square, scattering all who might have gotten in their path. Perhaps, thought Martin, my father is of the opinion that I will forget about the poor if I am kept away from them and my time is occupied by studies.

Martin soon discovered that changes had taken place while he was away. He had expected to go to his mother's adobe on Espíritu Santo, but he soon realized that the horses were carrying him to a different part of town. The houses, he noticed, were larger—there were no adobes—and some of them were built of colored stucco. Still the neighborhood was strange, and Martin was puzzled.

He trembled as a cold fear took hold of him. I wonder, he thought, if anything has happened to Mama? Martin closed his eyes and sat quietly until the horses stopped in front of a house he had never seen before.

"Wake up, Sleepyhead," Don Juan said playfully.

"Why have we stopped here?" the boy asked.

"This," Don Juan said, pointing to a comfortable-looking yellow stucco house surrounded by flowers and fruit trees, "is where you will live. I trust you will be much happier here than on Espíritu Santo."

Martin did not answer, nor did he make any effort to get out, though Don Juan instructed the driver to carry the boy's bags to the house. Then Don Juan himself stepped from the carriage.

"I must present my credentials to the Viceroy," he told Martin, and held out a hand to the boy.

"Mama—where is Mama?" Martin asked

quietly, without accepting the hand his father had extended.

"In time you will see her," Don Juan answered. "Come, the horses are getting restless."

"And you?" Martin had come to know his father well enough to understand that he must get all answers before they parted. "Will you not come with me to see what manner of house this is to which you have brought me?"

The look on Don Juan's face almost made Martin regret his words. The outstretched hand fell to the proud man's side. Martin's father knew there was no way to explain the gulf between Ana and himself without hurting their son. When the boy is older, Don Juan thought, he will understand how an open alliance between the governor of Panama and a woman so recently descended from African slaves would not be expected of one who is His Majesty's trusted servant and a Knight of Alcantara.

There were no further words between the father and son, but Martin stepped down from the carriage clutching a package Juana and Doña Lucita had sent his mother.

"It is already past the hour when I was expected to pay my respects to the Viceroy,"

Don Juan told the boy. "I shall see you before I put my head on a pillow tonight."

Martin watched his father's carriage drive away before he walked up the flower-path which led to the strange house where his father had said he would live. As he reached the door, it was opened suddenly and Martin found himself in his mother's arms.

Neither of them could find words to express their joy. Ana held her son close to her heart as if thanking God for bringing him back to her and begging that he not be taken away again. Then she made Martin turn round and round so she could see how he had grown.

The boy was stunned to find his mother in this strange house and a little ashamed of having doubted his father. He was to learn later that Doña Lucita and Don Diego had urged Don Juan to make provisions for Ana's support. As a result of the money which had been settled on her, she had been able to leave the poverty of Espíritu Santo behind and go to live with Francisca Velez Miquel, a woman known to Don Juan's family, who lived on the street called Malambo.

Yet Martin had known nothing of these changes until he found himself in his mother's arms. Though there was much he wished to know, Ana plied him with one question after another about Juana. He had to tell her all about Don Diego, Doña Lucita, and Anita. He had to describe the vast plantation and the many people who worked there.

When Señora Velez joined them, Ana was very proud of Martin's manners. When he showed his mother how he could write, he saw tears of happiness in her eyes, for Ana could barely sign her Christian name. Yet each time the boy mentioned his father he saw a shadow cross his mother's face and he knew that she, too, felt slighted because Don Juan had not stopped long enough to greet her.

"Don Juan has been appointed governor of Panama," Martin explained. "He will visit us after he has paid his respects to the Viceroy."

"That does not matter—any more," Ana told her son. "Now I have you."

"And Juana," Martin reminded.

"Juana will remain with her father's people. It is best that way."

Though Ana had smiled as she spoke, the boy knew it meant only that his mother had accepted the fact that her children's lives would follow a pattern far different from that of her own.

Don Juan kept his promise and returned that

night to the house on Malambo, though Martin
was asleep and his mother had to rouse him.
Don Juan promptly announced to Ana that he
was going to take Martin to Dr. Marcelo de
Rivero and make arrangements for the boy's
apprenticeship. When Ana made no comment,
Don Juan also told her that he intended to
see that Martin was confirmed before he left
for Panama. An awkward silence followed, and
Martin knew it was because again Don Juan
had made plans for the children without consulting their mother.

Martin left his parents alone and a short
while later heard a carriage drive off. His
mother came to his bed and, as she leaned over
him, he noticed for the first time that she was
aging. Though he pretended to be dozing, he
could see that the lines in her face were a little
deeper and that there were gray hairs which
he had not noticed before. Yet, Martin thought,
there was dignity in the way she held her head.
When the boy opened his eyes and stretched,
his mother was kneeling by the side of the bed.
Ana's smile was no longer troubled. When she
cradled the boy's face in her hands, he felt
happy and secure.

"You must promise that you will not blame
your father for anything." She spoke with

feeling. "By his kindness to you and Juana, he has—he has—"

"Mama, I understand what it is you find so hard to say. And I will promise what you ask. But I will also promise to make up to you for —for everything. And just think," the boy exclaimed, "I will be with you forever!"

"Forever is much too long a time," Ana warned, "and your *forever* may be tomorrow or whenever Dr. de Rivero accepts you as his apprentice."

"I will not have to leave you when I go to study to be a barber-surgeon," Martin insisted.

"Dr. de Rivero's shop is a great distance from Malambo," Ana pointed out. "You must live much nearer to him. But this will not mean that we will not see each other. Your father has already asked a lady who lives near the shop if you may stay with her while you are studying. I will visit you often."

Ana left the room before Martin could ask more questions about his father's most recent plan for his future. She did not want the boy to know how hurt she was over the arrangement which would take him away from her again. She had given her consent only after Don Juan had reminded her that it was all in the boy's best interests. She had heard of

Señora Ventura de Luna, with whom Martin would live, and she prayed that her son would be safe.

Before Don Juan sailed away from Peru, Martin was confirmed according to his father's wishes. Dr. de Rivero agreed to accept the boy as his apprentice and Martin was installed in the home of Señora Ventura de Luna. His sorrow over being separated from his mother and seeing his father sail away for Panama was softened by his discovery that this new home was only a short trot from the Church of San Lazaro and a few doors from the shop where he was to work and study.

CHAPTER *4*

Apprentice Surgeon

By the time Martin was twelve years old he was settled in his new home and had begun his studies with Dr. de Rivero. Each morning he went to the Church of San Lazaro, where he served Mass before he raced to the shop to have everything ready before the doctor arrived. Though it was only a matter of weeks before Martin's teacher decided that the boy

was as able a barber as he had ever instructed,
Marcelo de Rivero was surprised at the skill
with which Martin could also set broken limbs,
bind wounds, cool fevers and bleed patients.
Doubling as a barber-surgeon and compound-
ing potions for the sick left little time, but
Martin always managed to sweep the floors of
the shop, dust the shelves, and fill the jars
which held the drugs and herbs which Dr. de
Rivero used for healing the sick.

The shop consisted of three rooms: Dr. de
Rivero's office, a waiting room, and a larger
room, half barber shop and half pharmacy.
Though this alone was Martin's responsibility,
he soon came to know every patient who came
to see the doctor. The boy knew not only
their names but their ailments, and sometimes
they told him things they would hesitate to tell
the doctor. Dr. de Rivero chuckled over this
and said that now he had fewer complaints to
hear. The rotund, good-natured surgeon had
developed a fatherly affection for his friend's
son and he was proud of the way the boy took
to his profession.

Though the patients who crowded the shop
day after day came from all walks of life, it
was the poor to whom Martin was most atten-
tive. Whenever a woman or child looked hun-

gry, Martin managed to produce a piece of fruit, a loaf of bread or a handful of raisins. Several wealthy patients told the doctor that Martin had treated them in his absence, but had refused to accept payment, telling them to give the money to Dr. de Rivero. Some of them said that they had insisted on giving Martin a small gift of money, but that he would accept it only if it was understood that he would share it with poor friends or buy a gift for his mother. Whenever Martin was sent on an errand he always managed to find time to stop by the market place to leave fruit or bread for his friends.

Don Juan had left money with Dr. de Rivero for Martin's instruction, and after a time the boy was paid the usual apprentice's fee. Martin kept barely enough to pay for his lodging, however, and divided the rest between the poor and his mother, who visited him often and kept his clothing laundered and mended.

Señora de Luna liked the serious lad who had come to live with her, but after a while she began to wonder about him. She noticed that he seldom ate anything; the clothes he had brought from Quayaquil had become worn and shabby; and he seldom came home until several hours after the doctor's shop had closed. Upon inquiring, she learned that Martin went to the homes of patients who were too weak to come to the office and too poor to ask the doctor to visit them.

One morning, when she was setting her house in order, Martin made an unusual request. "Señora de Luna," he asked, "would you be kind enough to give me the stumps of the candles which you usually discard?"

The good woman was puzzled, but agreed. All that day she found herself thinking about Martin's request. Toward evening she gathered the accumulated candle stumps and went to his bare little room. A chair and table stood beside the bed. There were several books on the table: a medical book which Dr. de Rivero had lent Martin, and some lives of the saints.

"Books are so expensive that only the rich can afford them," Ventura de Luna mused, "and these must have cost Martin a great many pesos. Yet he will beg for the stumps of candles by which to read them. How he must love those books!"

Each night, regardless of how late she passed her lodger's room, and regardless of how late he had returned from his visits to the sick, there was always a faint ray of light under his door.

One morning, just before daybreak, a street noise awakened the Señora. As she went to the door to look out, she passed Martin's room and noticed a sliver of light under the door.

"That boy must have fallen asleep at his reading," the woman muttered. "I'd better wake him or he will not be fit for a day's work."

She knocked softly on Martin's door, but there was no answer. When she knocked the second time, she noticed that the door was slightly ajar.

"Martin! Martin!" she called. But the boy, kneeling before the crucifix he had hung on the wall over his bed the first day he came to live at her house, was in such a state of ecstasy that he did not hear her. He was bathed in a bright light which could never have come from the flickering candle.

Ventura de Luna's first impulse was to awaken the household and tell them what she had seen, but unconsciously she put her hand to her mouth, almost as if some unseen power had forced her to do so. "This boy is from God," she decided and from that moment on, though she never told Martin what she had seen, Ventura de Luna did all she could to help him.

Martin's day began before dawn. The Fathers at the Church of San Lazaro knew that he would be the first person in the church, waiting to serve Mass. Already he would have cleaned the barber shop and doctor's office.

Dr. de Rivero gave Martin some of his most difficult cases to test his knowledge and skill. There seemed no disease for which Martin did not remember a remedy, and no illness was too loathsome for him to lavish tender care on the sufferer. He would rush to help a poor Indian or Negro, who showed signs of having had no attention from a barber in months, in preference to the Spanish grandees who came to the shop with silver and gold coins jangling in their pockets.

Though Ana knew that it was best for Martin to live with Señora de Luna, nevertheless she grieved for her son. Sometimes she would not see him for a week; then she would awake one morning to find a basket of food inside her door and she would know that her son had visited while she slept. In her simple way, Ana marveled at this extraordinary son of hers. Already there was talk in the streets about people who had been helped in strange and almost miraculous ways.

Martin thought of his mother more than she

knew. He thought of his family in Quayaquil and wondered if Mass was being said in the little chapel by the gate. He knew that Anita and Doña Lucita must be pampering Juana, so he prayed that his sister would grow in wisdom and kindliness. There were times when a longing for all of them came upon him, but then he would turn his attention to the sick people waiting outside the shop each morning.

Dr. de Rivero was making house calls on a certain day as Martin busied himself setting the office in order. Noises from the street drifted in, and Martin wondered why so many people were astir at such an early hour. From time to time he went to the doorway and glanced at the crowd, singling out a few new faces among the familiar ones and noticing what appeared to be an argument between two Indians.

Martin looked up at the sky. The low-hanging storm clouds must be affecting their dispositions, he thought, as he hurried back to his sweeping. He was dusting the shelves when a clap of thunder rolled across the sky. As he stood still for a moment, listening, the angry voices of the two men arguing rose above all the rest.

There was no mistaking the fact that a violent argument was in progress just outside the office door. There was another peal of thunder, a volley of curses, and then a piercing scream, louder than either the thunder or the curses.

Martin ran to the doorway, pushed his way through the crowd, and saw one of the Indians lying crumpled up at the bottom of the steps as blood poured from a deep gash across his forehead. Standing over the writhing form was the other Indian, still holding the blood-stained knife.

Martin knew that he would have to work fast or the man would bleed to death. He tore a piece of cloth from the bottom of his shirt, asked one of the bystanders to hold it to the wounded man's forehead, and ran inside to get a basin of water and a sponge. He paused before a shelf, trying to decide which herb he should put in the water as an antiseptic and which powder would be best to stanch the flow of blood. Please, dear God, Martin prayed, help me to make the right choice. Suddenly his eyes lit on two jars he had not yet replaced on the shelf after dusting—and they were the very two he needed. He took a bottle of brandy, for good measure, and rushed outside.

An angry sun broke through the clouds and beat down on Martin as he knelt beside the bleeding Indian. Martin's lips moved in prayer as he bathed the wound, but the blood continued to flow. One of the beggars fanned the young apprentice with a small leafy branch torn from a near-by tree.

Once more Martin went into the office for water and bandages. When he came back, the patient was making a gurgling sound.

"He's dying," an old woman screamed. "He's dying! I hear the death rattle."

"He will not die unless it is God's will," Martin said firmly.

He bent over the wounded man again, and then the frown on his face became an expression of puzzlement that turned into a smile as he saw that there was only a thin trickle of blood oozing from the wound. The crowd moved in closer as they sensed the change in Martin. He motioned to the beggar to fetch more water, and once again he bathed the wound and covered it with the healing powder.

Then Martin waited. He had done all he could. The rest, he knew, was up to God.

The wounded man shuddered and opened his eyes. Martin saw happily that not one drop of blood had penetrated the thick coating of powder. He took the bandage from his pocket and bound the Indian's head before helping him to his feet with a reassuring pat.

The crowd fell back as if they feared the wounded man had been crazed and might turn upon them at any moment. When nothing happened and Martin began speaking softly to his patient, they drew near again.

"You will be all right now," the young apprentice told the Indian, taking from another pocket the small bottle of brandy for which he would have to pay Doctor de Rivero. "If you feel weak, drink some of this, and go in peace."

The Indian and his friends tried to kiss Martin's hand as they thanked him over and over for what he had done.

"Thank God," he told the Indian. "If you had been stabbed anywhere else, you might have bled to death before help could have reached you. It is to God you must be grateful for this!"

This did not stop the bystanders from saying that Martin had performed a miracle. When Dr. de Rivero came back, some of them were still standing around the pool of blood where the man had first fallen. The doctor questioned Martin, but the young apprentice explained that he had only treated the wound as the doc-

tor had taught him. Soon the office was filled
with patients, and Marcelo de Rivero could
see that he would have more than a day's share
of sick babies to treat. There was no time to
wonder about miracles.

Wherever the young apprentice went, he
was followed by children who knew that he
carried fruit and raisins in his pockets. Late
one evening, after he had finished his visits to
the sick, as he neared the house of Señora de
Luna he heard a man screaming curses at a
group of boys. They were children of the
streets, and Martin knew that many of them
lived wherever they found a place to sleep and
ate whatever was available. Now they crowded
around Martin for protection as one of them
explained that they were hungry and had taken
lemons from one of several trees in the man's
yard.

Martin told the man that the boys had eaten
his lemons because they had nothing else to
eat and went on to ask, almost playfully, if the
man would give him a limb from one of the
trees.

"What do you want with a limb?" the
owner asked suspiciously.

"I only want to plant it," Martin told him.

"When it bears fruit, the boys will no longer molest you. Have no fear; you can trust me."

Anxious to be rid of all of them, the man gave Martin a tiny switch from one of the lemon trees. Martin told the boys to follow him to the yard outside Ventura de Luna's house. There he stuck the plant in the ground, made the sign of the Cross, and told the boys that the sapling would grow so fast that it would bear fruit before the year had passed. The urchins laughed because they thought Martin was trying to make them forget that there were more lemons in the grove from which they had been stealing. Strangely enough, they found that they had already lost their desire for the stolen lemons.

Whenever Martin met the boys, he usually had a piece of fruit or some tidbit to share with them. No one asked about the tree, and he knew that they had all forgotten until one day he asked them to come and see it. On the spot where he had planted the sapling was a small lemon tree, its branches drooping from the burden of yellow fruit.

The people of Lima learned about "Martin's lemon tree" and it is said that fifty years after his death it was still bearing fruit.

As Martin's fame spread, his need for food and money to give the poor increased. He ate next to nothing, in order to be able to share his food with the hungry. His clothes were almost in rags. Sometimes Señora de Luna or his mother would sew up a torn shirt for him or patch his pants, but it made no difference to Martin how he looked as long as his body was covered. He gave a part of his salary to his mother, and he continued to buy books, for most of his nights were spent in spiritual reading and prayer.

Martin never refused to care for the rich patients who came to Dr. de Rivero's office—indeed, many of them clamored for the attention of the mulatto boy, as they heard of his success in curing his patients—but Martin continued to feel that the poor people needed him more. As the richest men in Lima sought his services, Dr. de Rivero urged Martin to accept some of the gifts they pressed upon him. He did accept some, but it was soon evident by his shabby appearance that the money went from his pockets to the unfortunate ones who depended upon him.

Regardless of the section of the city Martin had to visit, he always found a church. One of his favorite places of prayer was the beautiful Church of the Queen of the Most Holy Rosary. Martin, in his shabby clothes, with his surgeon's kit beside him, was often seen kneeling before the Blessed Sacrament in this church. It followed in a natural way that he sought out the Dominican priests in the near-by Convent of the Holy Rosary for advice on some of the spiritual matters which troubled him.

When Martin told them of his distress because people thought he had cured them of their illnesses, not realizing that their help had come from God, the Dominicans knew that he was no ordinary boy. He spoke freely of his love for the poor, his desire to atone for the sins which had nailed Our Lord to the Cross, and the hot temper which he prayed so hard to control. It was clear to the priests that this lad already bore the mark of sanctity.

Though some time was still to pass before Martin made the decision which was to alter the course of his life, his Dominican friends were destined to bolster his courage during the trying days he had to face.

CHAPTER 5

A New Way of Life

During the long nights at Señora de Luna's,
Martin knelt before the crucifix and asked
himself what he could do to atone for the sins
of the world. He longed to spend every hour
of every day in penance and prayer. Yet if
he did this he would have no money or time
to share with his poor friends. The conflict

65

plunged him into spells of deep depression. He resolved to see if the Dominican Fathers could help him.

"I need your help, Padre," Martin told Prior Francisco Vega, as he stood in the parlor of Holy Rosary Convent. Father Vega listened as Martin discussed his spiritual life and the doubts that plagued him. Obviously this was an extraordinary boy, as the priest had known the first time the young apprentice came to talk with him. Now the prior went to get Father de Lorenzano, the Provincial, and together they explained to Martin that the devil is untiring in his efforts to steal exceptional souls from God. Undoubtedly Martin was going through a period when Satan was redoubling his efforts. Perhaps, they suggested, God might have a special mission for Martin. This thought seemed to startle the boy, and he quickly concluded the conversation with hasty good-bys.

After Martin left, the two priests agreed that there were indeed signs of a religious vocation. They could not help but realize, too, that if God were leading Martin toward the Dominican Order, as He seemed to be doing, they would have need of great wisdom and tact. The sons of some of the noblest Spanish families of Peru had found their life's work within the order—but this boy, Martin, was a half-breed surgeon's apprentice. What problems might this situation present? Ah well, they would leave it in God's hands. Meanwhile, they must pray for guidance.

Martin, too, prayed for guidance, and after many nights of prayer and intense soul-searching, the boy knew what he wanted to do. Again he presented himself at the Convent of the Holy Rosary. He told Father de Lorenzano that he would live at the convent as a tertiary, a lay helper.

The Provincial studied the radiant face of the boy. Surely, he thought, men of noble birth will not begrudge him the right to be a lowly tertiary.

When Martin told his mother of his decision, she was troubled. Should not the son of Don Juan de Porres be more than a mere helper to the priests? She knew that Don Juan had high hopes for Martin and would spare no expense to further his education as a surgeon. She also feared his hot temper when he felt that his pride had been trampled.

Ana did not have long to live with her fears, for quite unexpectedly Martin's father arrived in Lima on business for the king. Don

Juan went to the house on Malambo where Ana lived soon after he left the boat, for he was anxious for news of Martin. When Ana told him that his son was now making preparations to enter the convent as a Dominican tertiary, he was furious.

"If that is so," he exclaimed, "the son of Don Juan de Porres should be no less than a priest!" And Don Juan went to the Convent of the Holy Rosary for a conference with the Provincial and the Prior, who were both known to him.

They sent for Martin. "I am not worthy to be a priest," the boy insisted, in answer to his father's objections. "I only want to serve God in the ways I can."

"As a tertiary you will be nothing more than a servant," Don Juan declared. "If you must do this thing, then at least become a lay brother—a professed religious."

When Martin begged to be allowed to do what he believed to be the will of God, the Dominicans called Don Juan aside and urged him to allow the boy to do what he thought best.

Fifteen-year-old Martin was up before dawn the day he was to enter the Convent of the

Most Holy Rosary. After Mass he hurried to the market place to say good-by to his friends, thinking that they would share his happiness, but he soon found that he was wrong. The beggars, whose faces usually gladdened at the sound of Martin's footsteps, sat silent with bowed heads, even after he had spoken to them.

"I will attend to my shopping," he decided. "Perhaps fruits and bread will loosen their tongues." The boy was making his way to the stall of a fruit merchant when an old woman, crouched near the shop, threw her arms about his legs.

"Why are you leaving me?" she wailed. "I have nobody to care for me but you. Now you are going to that convent."

"I am not leaving you," Martin tried to explain, as he realized why the beggars were so dejected. "Don't you know the Convent of the Holy Rosary? You will find me there whenever you have need of me. Please," he called out to those who sat with bowed heads, "this is a time for rejoicing, not for weeping."

The old woman wailed louder than ever. Martin turned toward the others, but they looked away with tears in their eyes. All over the city Martin found his friends huddled in small groups, sharing their misery with each other. After a while he realized that his words of comfort were wasted. He left a basket of food where the beggars might find it when hunger chased away their grief, and returned to Dr. de Rivero's office.

He packed his instruments and then decided to pay a last call on some of his most serious cases, for he did not know when he might attend them again. Leaving the office, he met a lad of seven or eight, who had known no other doctor but Martin. Martin reached into his pocket and offered the boy a sweet, as had been his custom, but the child burst into tears. "Why are you leaving us?" he asked.

Martin rested his bundle of belongings and put his arm about the boy. "I am not leaving you. I am only going to the Convent of the Holy Rosary to work in the infirmary. I will have more food, more medicine, and twice as many prayers to give you as ever before. Will you promise to help me by doing just as I tell you?"

The boy wiped his eyes and listened as Martin told him how to reach the convent by the quickest path. "You must watch out for the old people and the sick," he told his little

helper, "and lead them to the convent whenever they need me."

As Martin spoke, his mind raced ahead of
his words as he planned how he would save
food for his friends by putting aside some of
his own food in the refectory.

"You must run along and spread the good
news among all our friends," Martin told the
boy. "Tell them that they should be happy
because I will have more time to thank Him
who has given me all I have shared with them.
And be sure to tell them that you will bring
them to me whenever they need me."

The child ran off smiling.

As Martin approached the convent, he began
to have misgivings. Doctor de Rivero had
wanted to come along, but Martin had insisted
on going alone. His knees were trembling as
he walked through the courtyard. A fountain
stood in the center of it, and Martin stopped
for a moment to admire the floating water-
lilies. The tiled verandas of the yellow stone
convent building face out on the courtyard.

"Perhaps I won't even have strength enough
to ring the bell," thought Martin as he
approached the main doorway.

But he need not have worried about ringing

the bell. The Prior had seen him in the courtyard and now came to the door with a smile of
welcome on his lips.

It was a happy beginning, and Martin was
quickly set to work at various chores throughout the convent. He was to be called Brother
Martin, even though he was not a lay brother,
and was given the white tunic of the Dominican tertiary. A rosary hung about his neck, and
another from his belt. Over and over Martin
would finger the beads around his neck and
whisper to himself: "Slaves wear chains, and if
I can prove myself worthy, I can be a slave
to Our Lady."

The day Martin was assigned to the convent barbershop, the Prior explained that the
Dominican Rule required that hair be cut very
close all around the head. Brother Martin had
followed instructions and had successfully cut
the hair of several priests and brothers when
Brother James sat down to have his hair cut.
Brother James was the son of a wealthy family
and, though he was yet only a student for the
priesthood, he never forgot that there were
few of his brethren who could boast of having
descended from such eminent forebears.

Brother James read a book while Martin
cut his hair. When a bell rang to call him to

his next class, he jumped up. As he ran a hand over his closely cropped head, he gasped. "What have you done?" he exclaimed angrily. "There is almost nothing left! Don't you know that people from good families wear their hair long on the sides? But then, how could *you* know about good families? This is what comes of taking men like you into a decent house."

"Brother James, I am sorry that I have displeased you," Martin began. "I have cut your hair according to the Rule—short all around."

"How dare you tell *me* about the Rule!" Brother James sneered.

Martin knew that he could have defended himself, but what an opportunity this was to make a small payment on the great debt he owed his crucified Lord! "Dear Brother James," he said humbly, "forgive me. Here is a fresh orange that was given to me. Please accept it."

Brother James snatched the orange from Martin and strode off in a huff, leaving the barber to wait humbly for his next customer.

As Martin was especially kind to the novices, he became interested in the case of Brother Francisco Velasco, a young student who was suffering from dropsy. Raging with fever, he

grew weaker by the day. Finally the doctor
had him locked in a room alone, lest his great
thirst drive him to seek water and thus hasten
his death. The doctor and the priests had given
up all hope of saving Francisco's life; alone
in his cell, he felt abandoned and miserable.

As the night wore on, the sick man's pain
increased. His cell was cold, and his thirst so
great that he felt he could not live much
longer without water. The bedclothes were
damp and uncomfortable. Death seemed to be
his only chance of relief. He closed his eyes
and pressed his lips to keep from crying out in
pain.

About one o'clock in the morning, the sick
man had the strange feeling that he was not
alone. "This is foolish," he muttered to himself. "The door is locked and bolted." Then,
with a deep sigh, he opened his eyes to see
Brother Martin leaning over him.

At first Brother Velasco thought he was
dreaming, but when he felt the cloth of
Martin's habit he knew that he was not. "How
did you get in here, Brother Martin?" he
asked. "The door is bolted, and only the
Novice Master has a key."

"You must not be too talkative." Martin

smiled and brought fresh linens, herbs, and a pan of burning coals to dispel the cold. A peaceful sensation settled upon Francisco as Martin bathed him, changed the bed linen, and sprinkled the sheets with fragrant rosemary. By now Francisco's thirst had left him, but his limbs were still bloated. He looked at Martin with questioning eyes.

"You are not going to die," Martin said, "for already you are much better."

"I can't understand," the novice murmured. He was free from pain, but exhausted. He closed his eyes for a second, then remembered that he had not properly thanked Martin. When he opened his eyes, the room was empty. Brother Velasco drifted off into a peaceful sleep.

The next morning Brother Velasco excitedly told the Novice Master about Martin's visit. "You must have been dreaming, my son," was the reply. "The key to this room has not been out of my possession." But he examined the young man carefully and then hurriedly summoned the doctor, who confirmed that there were no longer any signs of the disease. Brother Velasco was allowed to get up, completely cured. Many years later, after Martin's death, he told the story to a court which had met to gather facts on Martin's life. By that time, Martin's ability to open doors without keys was better understood.

The novices at the Convent of the Holy Rosary had a special fondness for Martin, and he for them. If ever a young novice needed a friend, it was Cypriano de Medina. He was short and stocky, with a coarse face and manners which caused his companions to call him *El Bruto*, the brute. He was not a good student, and some of the novices said that he was downright stupid.

One day, when Cypriano had been the butt of a number of jokes made by his companions, Martin surprised some of the novices by declaring, "You call Cypriano an ugly brute because he is clumsy, but he will turn out to be a fine young man and will bring great honor to the Order of Preachers."

Some years later Cypriano became critically ill. He lay in the infirmary as Brother Martin rushed about taking care of other patients but seldom going near Cypriano. Finally the young man could bear this neglect no longer, for he had always felt that Brother Martin liked and understood him, even if no one else did.

He called out, "Brother Martin, why do you

abandon me, when you know that I am so ill and may even die?"

Martin smiled. "Cypriano," he said, "you ought to know me well enough to be reassured by my apparent neglect. Don't you know that when I visit a sick person it is often a sign that he will not recover? So, my son, be of good cheer. The Lord intends to prolong your life for His glory, the salvation of souls, and the honor of our holy order."

Cypriano was ill for a long time, and when he did recover his appearance was so altered that he scarcely seemed to be the same man. No longer was he ugly and coarse-looking. His clothes were too small, for now he was several inches taller. Most astounding of all, this novice who had once been called stupid made remarkable progress in his studies. He continued to advance spiritually as well as intellectually, became Regent of Studies at the University of Lima, and eventually Bishop of Huamanga. Martin's prophecy had been fulfilled and his prayers for the "ugly novice" had been answered. Indeed, the miracle of Cypriano's transformation had been so well concealed that it almost appeared to be the result of the passing years.

Martin had been given or had assumed so many duties that soon he was doing the work of several men. His superiors decided to make him infirmarian-in-charge, in order to relieve him of most of the other work he had taken upon himself. Being official infirmarian at this convent was a position of great responsibility, for there were nearly 300 priests, Brothers, tertiaries, and servants living in the house. Moreover, it was the custom to bring to Holy Rosary the sick from the neighboring Dominican Convent of St. Mary Magdalen. In addition, the workers at Limatambo, the convent's plantation, had a separate wing in the hospital.

The Provincial and Prior soon realized that instead of shortening Martin's work day, the new assignment had only spurred him on to a point which would have exhausted any other man. Sometimes his companions found him in the chapel, asleep in front of the Blessed Sacrament. In the chapter hall and in the infirmary he had a special bench where he sometimes stretched out for the few hours of sleep he allowed himself, instead of going to his cell where his bed was a crude bunk with a stone for a pillow.

Once when the energetic infirmarian had himself contracted a stubborn fever, the Prior

ordered Martin to go to bed and insisted that
he should provide himself with sheets and a
blanket, luxuries he seldom allowed himself.
Martin obeyed promptly but he went to bed
without removing his clothes or his shoes. Next
to his skin he wore a horsehair shirt, and his
tunic was of the roughest woolen serge.

When one of the priests discovered that
Martin had gone to bed fully clothed, he
reported it to the Prior. But the wise superior
forbade anyone to reprimand the infirmarian.
"Martin is a good theologian," he said. "He
knows the secret of uniting obedience with
mortification."

It soon became clear to his superiors that
Martin would not be deterred from his endless
works of charity. No task was too tiring or
too menial. He devoted himself body and soul
to Holy Rosary Convent—and his superiors
found, to their amazement, that the entire city
of Lima was not too large to fall into his
embrace.

CHAPTER 6

Miracle Man of Peru

As soon as the news spread among the towns-
people that Brother Martin could be found in
Holy Rosary infirmary, the sick and the poor
began making their way to the convent. The
infirmary soon looked like the clinic of a city
hospital. Some could only hobble and others
had to be carried, but their one desire was to

get to Brother Martin, who they were sure could cure them. Others came who were not ill; poverty was their only affliction. But whether it was food or clothing they sought, Martin found some means to send them away with more than they brought. The infirmary became a clinic, dispensary and welfare center combined, and the name of Brother Martin was spoken with love and reverence wherever the poor people of Lima gathered.

Martin continued to go both to the Dominican plantation at Limatambo and to the streets and market place of Lima. The Indians and Negroes who worked on the plantation looked forward to Martin's visits at Limatambo. Instead of resting, he cared for the sick on the property, then went into the neighboring countryside to look after those he had heard were ailing. Not only did he clean their bodies and dress their wounds, he taught these workers to adopt more hygienic methods of living so as to avoid disease. They had great confidence in his wisdom, and he counseled them on matters both temporal and spiritual. When they were beset by fears and Martin did not appear at Limatambo when they needed advice, they found some way of getting to Lima to see him.

When Brother Martin walked the streets of

Lima, a procession of children and animals followed him. Everybody with a special problem ran to meet this wisest of friends and ask his advice. Even lovers confided in him concerning affairs of the heart.

Some of Martin's friends who came to the convent infirmary seeking help needed more attention than he could give them in one day, so he began to take special cases to his cell where he could treat them and watch them through the night.

As Martin took more and more special cases to his cell, his fellow-religious began to feel that their privacy was being invaded. The Provincial agreed to take steps to control Martin's excessive charity. He told Martin that he would have to restrict his nursing to the infirmary; no more special cases were to be housed anywhere else in the convent.

The years had brought many changes. Ana Velasquez lived to see her son acclaimed for his charitable works. She lived for many years with Señora Velez Miquel, seeing her son often, but inevitably the day came when she was fatally stricken. The Provincial sent Martin to the house on Malambo, which he entered to find Señora Velez weeping beside Ana's body. Martin had a deep affection for his mother and he knew that her life had been a hard one. Though she had long since forgiven Don Juan for his neglect, the separation from Juana and Martin was a cross she bore daily.

Sorrows often follow one upon the other. Soon after Ana's death, a plague swept through Ecuador. Of those that Martin had loved best, only Juana and her nurse Anita were spared. Through the help of a priest who lived near Don Diego's estate, the two were brought to Lima where Don Juan established them in a comfortable house just outside the city. It was to this house that Juana, ever the devoted little sister, told Martin to bring his emergency cases after the Provincial had forbidden him to care for them in his room.

One day when Martin was returning to the convent from Juana's, he stumbled over something in the road. A closer look revealed the form of an Indian who had been stabbed and left in the road to die. Martin saw at a glance that the man was losing a great deal of blood; he could not live much longer. Martin made a bandage out of the man's shirt and applied it above the wound to stop the bleeding. Then he began to wonder where he could take him. It was too far to Juana's house, and he had been forbidden to care for patients in his room in the convent. "It seems that I have no choice," thought Martin. "Either I take him to the convent and put him in my cell, or he dies."

Even the short trip to the convent started the wound bleeding again. When Martin got the man to his cell, he stopped the blood, washed the wound, and treated it with an ointment from the infirmary. He was too weak to be moved and Martin made him comfortable for the night, thinking he would take him to his sister's house the next day.

Unfortunately, someone discovered Martin's patient and the matter was reported to the Prior, who sent for Martin and reminded him of the rules. Martin made no effort to justify his act and cheerfully carried out a severe penance. The Indian recovered and went on his way.

A few days later Martin was performing some small service for the Prior. When he had finished, he knelt before his superior and asked his blessing, explaining that he was very sorry for having been disobedient.

Touched by Martin's contrition, the Prior replied, "You are forgiven, Brother Martin, but I really found it necessary to punish you for disobeying a regulation which I consider necessary for the well-being of the priory."

"Forgive my mistake, dear Father," Martin said, "but please be good enough to set me straight on this question. Was I wrong in thinking that the precept of obedience yielded in such an emergency to the demands of charity and mercy?"

It was clear to the Prior that Martin had considered himself justified in bringing the dying Indian into the convent in order to save his life. He was impressed by Martin's intense desire to be obedient and, at the same time, care for all of God's creatures. "From now on," he told Martin, "use your own judgement in such cases." Though there was some grumbling in the convent, everybody was forced to respect the Prior's wishes.

Brother Thomas was one of Martin's most cherished friends at the Convent of the Holy Rosary, and when he fell ill the infirmarian spared no pains in caring for him. There were always a number of homeless boys who lived at the convent, so Martin assigned one of them to sleep in Brother Thomas's room. Then he would be sure that his friend was never unattended.

One morning the boy ran out of the sick-room screaming, "Brother Thomas is dead!" Martin and several others rushed to see; Brother Thomas's body was indeed stiff and cold. As the other members of the community gathered outside the door, Martin began to prepare the body for burial. As his eyes fell upon the crucifix at the head of Brother Thomas's bed, he felt an overpowering urge to beg God for the life of this friend. Already he could hear his brethren saying the prayers for the dead.

Brother Fernando of Aragon, the porter, was standing near by to assist if necessary. Martin ordered him to go out and close the door. Then he threw himself on his knees before the crucifix.

After praying earnestly, Martin called out, "Brother Thomas!"

Unknown to Martin, Brother Fernando had not left the room but had hidden in a closet to see what Martin would do. When Fernando heard him call to Brother Thomas and then heard the dead man make a gagging sound, he came out of hiding to make sure that his ears were not playing tricks.

Once more Martin called, "Brother Thomas!" The still form twitched and a sigh escaped the body.

Martin called Brother Thomas's name a third time. Fernando watched Thomas's lips move and eyelids flutter.

Brother Fernando could no longer be quiet. "Oh, how wonderful is Almighty God," he exclaimed, "to restore life to the dead through the prayers of His holy servant!"

Martin threw open the door. "God be praised!" he called to the religious outside the room. "Brother Thomas has fortunately regained consciousness. Now you may go back to your cells."

Many years later, when Brother Fernando had become a priest, he swore under oath to the details of this event. He testified that after Brother Thomas began to breathe Martin sent him to get the boiled yolk of three fresh eggs, and together they fed the sick man until he regained complete consciousness.

Martin's miracles of healing were not limited to his Dominican brothers. His good friends among the laity shared in the benefits.

When Doña Isabel Ortiz fell ill from severe hemorrhage, the doctors feared for her life. The woman sent for Martin and begged him to pray for her. Martin knelt beside her bed for some time; then he rose from his knees and told Doña Isabel that he was quite certain she would not die from this illness. He then pulled an apple from his pocket and urged her to eat. The sick woman hesitated, but Martin told her it was important that she follow his directions. Doña Isabel did as Martin told her and in five days was restored to perfect health.

Another of Martin's friends, Don Juan de Figueroa, who had helped Martin with many of his charities, was stricken suddenly with a deadly throat infection. Martin was very fond of Don Juan, so it was with some concern that he hurried to his bedside. After a long visit, Martin assured Don Juan that he should not despair. Then he left a bottle on a near-by table and asked to be excused for a few minutes. Don Juan thought that Martin would return. He waited for some time. When it became apparent that Martin had gone, Don Juan became curious about the bottle on the table. It looked and smelled like water. Suddenly Don Juan was inspired to drink from the bottle, and immediately his throat was healed. While he could barely whisper before, he cried out for Brother Martin in a loud voice. One of the women servants, seeing what had happened to her master, bathed her face in the water which was left in the bottle and was immediately cured of a skin disease which had disfigured her for years.

Still the wonders continued. Doña Francisca, wife of a good man who often contributed to Martin's charities, fell ill with a malady which her chemist husband, Don Mateo, could not identify. He dispatched his servants to all sections of the city in search of doctors. After all of the physicians had gathered and examined Doña Francisca, none of them seemed to know what was wrong with her. In spite of the medicines they prescribed, she grew so weak that her husband feared she would not live through the day. The doctors were still consulting when Don Mateo looked up to see Brother Martin in the doorway of Doña Francisca's room.

"I just stopped by for a visit," said Martin casually as he touched Don Mateo's shoulder affectionately.

Glaring at Martin as if he were an intruder, the doctors went to stand at one end of the room while Martin approached the bed. Doña Francisca opened her eyes. Though her lips moved, no one could hear what she was trying to say. Her husband and the doctors watched as she raised her hand and took hold of Brother Martin's habit. At the very instant the clothing touched her body, Doña Francisca's breathing became normal. Every eye in the room was watching as the color returned to her cheeks and the woman who had seemed in the throes of death a few moments before sat up in bed.

"Oh, what a great servant of God you are, Brother Martin!" were her first words.

Embarrassed, Martin replied: "It is God who has done this, Señora—God and the holy habit of our Father Dominic. Give thanks to God, for I am merely an instrument in His hands, chosen to bring consolation to you. Of myself I am only a sinner, unworthy of the holy habit which I wear. May God be blessed for his merciful kindness to you."

In 1603, when Martin was twenty-four years of age, in obedience to a direct order from his superiors, he agreed to become a lay brother. No longer was he to be merely a tertiary living in the Convent of the Holy Rosary, but a professed religious, a member of the Dominican Order. Besides his habit, Martin could now wear the cloak and capuche or hood.

Brother Martin's superiors had learned that there was little need to tell him what work he was to do. He had assumed numerous duties, all of which he discharged so well that it seemed miraculous for one man to accomplish so much.

Everybody knew that Martin rang the bell for
Matins and for Vespers. They saw him sweeping the cloisters each day. He cut hair and
shaved, then took care of the infirmary. The
sick and poor waited at the convent gate until
he came to care for them, and whenever there
was some lowly task that everybody else
shunned, Martin was the one who did it. His
pleasant smile and kind words brought happiness to all whose lives he touched, whether
they were in the convent or outside in the city.

Many notables visited the Convent of the
Holy Rosary to talk with Brother Martin. One
who held this humble lay brother in great es-
teem was Don Feliciano de la Vego, Archbishop of Mexico. Martin's companions sometimes reminded him that the Archbishop would
probably be happy to grant him special privi-
leges, and even asked him to use his influence
on their behalf, but Martin refused to listen to
such suggestions.

When one of the brothers asked Martin, as
he was cleaning one day, "Brother, wouldn't
you prefer to be taking your ease in the palace
of the Archbishop of Mexico than to be here
engaged in such a menial occupation?", Martin
merely laughed and said that he had no wish
for any other place in life.

Martin was more concerned with his constant battle to control his quick temper than with any thought of worldly honor. Nothing but the memory of Our Lord's suffering on the Cross had prevented him from using his surgeon's knife to avenge some of the insults hurled at him. Thus, when praises fell on his ears, he flogged his pride with the knowledge of that inner struggle.

He seized every opportunity for mortification as, when one of his fellow religious, in a fit of temper, called him a "dog of a mulatto" and said that he deserved only to be a galley-slave.

To the astonishment of all who were present, Martin knelt before the man and tried to kiss his feet, as he said, "I deserve much more for my wicked deeds, and I know well what a miserable creature I am."

What seemed to be an insult was to Martin de Porres but one more step toward Calvary.

Martin's devotion to the Mother of God increased with the passing years. He was constantly fingering the beads around his neck or the rosary which hung at his waist. Each morning at four o'clock he climbed the steps to the bell tower and greeted the dawn with bells which pealed in honor of the Blessed Virgin. Before her statue at the entrance to the refectory, Martin placed fresh flowers and lighted candles each day. The Little Office of the Blessed Virgin was among his daily prayers and he loved to meditate on the mysteries of the rosary, reliving the scenes of Our Lord's life.

Though Martin knew he was but an instrument of God and tried to conceal the wonders and cures which resulted from his prayers, Our Lord stamped His servant with His approval in such a way that all became aware of his holiness. One night during the recitation of Matins, the entire Dominican community noticed a bright light shining in the vicinity of the main altar. They found Martin kneeling in a recess so as to avoid attention, completely lost in ecstasy, his countenance bathed in a light of celestial splendor.

CHAPTER **7**

Father to the Poor

As the days of Martin's youth passed, he became truly a father to the poor of Lima. His charities were aided by circumstances which might seem to us contradictory. It is true that most of the Spanish adventurers were driven on by the hunger for gold, but they were also given to spurts of generosity. In spite of the cruelties they inflicted, the Spaniards also gave financial support to the missionaries' efforts to convert the people who had inhabited the New World before they arrived, as well as Negro slaves brought from Africa. The conscience of the Spanish grandee did not let him forget that the man he enslaved was endowed with an immortal soul. Most historians are of the opinion that the early Spanish settlers in the New World showed more concern for the spiritual welfare of the natives than did any of the other pioneers who came to North America.

Martin knew many of the rich men in Lima, for when disease struck they called for him as quickly as did the poor. They showed their appreciation for Martin's care by giving him substantial gifts. Knowing the needs of the people as he did, and always full of plans for new projects if only he had the money to carry them out, Martin drove a hard bargain with these men. Amused and impressed by Martin's shrewdness on behalf of his poor, the merchants of Lima often gave him many times what he asked for.

Nothing made Martin so sad as to be unable to help the poor. If he encountered a needy person at a moment when he had no money, he would sell or pawn his clothing or possessions. At least twice he took the cloak from his own back to give to a beggar. When occasionally Martin found himself with neither money nor something to sell, he increased his already strenuous penances, begging God to provide for the poor.

Martin's partners in charity were Brother John Masias and his well-known donkey. Brother John was attached to the neighboring Dominican Convent of St. Mary Magdalen. St. John the Apostle had appeared to him when he was a very young man in Spain, John once told Martin. The saint had urged his namesake to go to Peru, where the young brother began his works of charity. Brother John lived a holy life and was beatified with Brother Martin in 1836.

Equally well known was "Brother John's donkey," who regularly walked alone through the city streets wearing a saddlebag which Brother John had strapped on. Generous almsgivers put food and money in the donkey's bag, and when it was full the faithful animal would return to his master.

"Small wonder that no thief has stolen from my donkey twice," Brother John used to say. "Sad to recall, anyone known to make a second try has usually met with some unfortunate accident—a sudden dizzy spell, perhaps, or a smashed finger."

The two Dominicans enjoyed a pleasant secret conspiracy, and a rich grandee who avoided making contributions to one was sure to be approached by the other. If one of Brother John's poor friends needed medical help, he sent for Martin; if Martin heard that the soldiers garrisoned at Callao, for instance, were without food and necessities, Brother John and his donkey were asked to accompany him on the long journey over the rough road to Callao.

The two Brothers were often companions in prayer as well as in charity. Occasionally Martin would send a boy to St. Mary Magdalen's to see if Brother John could join him in the garden of Holy Rosary Convent. This quiet sanctuary at the far end of the property was enclosed by a high, brick wall which shielded the friars from curious passers-by.

Martin would wait for Brother John in the garden, breathing in the scent of the flowering trees and shrubs. He loved to stand here and look at the beautiful stone convent, built with the gold of the Spanish grandees. It was a fine example of the architecture of its day. Tiled verandas encircled the patio with its fountain, and Martin thought that the only inharmonious feature was the wing which had been built on one end. He loved every corridor, every stairway, every nook of Holy Rosary Convent.

When Brother John arrived, the two would go off to the most remote corner they could find, sometimes looking like overgrown boys playing hide-and-seek as they took refuge in the shadow of a bush or behind a tree, where they could not be seen from the convent. Then they would hang a picture of Our Lord on a limb and spend long hours kneeling in prayer and contemplation.

In many of Martin's charities his sister Juana, who was now married, was a silent partner. Her loyalty was all the more admirable because Martin's zeal had caused her some uneasy moments before her marriage. When Juana returned to Lima from Quayaquil, Martin had been given the sum of two thousand pesos for his sister's dowry. By that time, Martin's reputation had grown to such an extent that everywhere he went he was confronted by people in need of food, clothing or shelter. He went from one merchant to the other, but in order to provide for all who sought his help he was obliged from time to time to use money from the sum he had been given for Juana's dowry.

Juana herself heard so much about Martin's generosity that she began to wonder where he was getting so much money, but she did not dream that he was using her dowry. As the time for Juana's marriage approached, however, Martin had to admit to his sister that he had used her dowry to feed and clothe the poor people of Lima. Her grief was a severe punishment to Martin and he prayed to be able to replace the money as quickly as possible. A wealthy friend heard of his predicament and gave Martin the two thousand pesos. Juana, who in spite of her grief had never rebuked her brother, was delighted, and the marriage came off as planned.

Martin's charities extended even to prisoners in the city jail. One day, as he was walking by, he saw two prisoners peering out of a window.

"Brother Martin," one of them cried, "we are almost dead from hunger. Won't you bring us a loaf of bread?"

Martin stopped and listened as the other prisoners took up the cry for bread. He had no money, no food, and nothing to sell. At that moment, as he stepped over a puddle of water, he saw a reflection of his image. Until then, he had forgotten that he was wearing a hat.

Martin hurried to a merchant with whom he often traded. When he left the store he was minus a hat, but he had pesos in his pocket. Off he went to the market place, where he bought bread and fruit, and then back to the jail. The prisoners crowded around the small window facing the street and tried to stretch their hands through the bars for the food which they knew Martin was bringing, for they were afraid the jailer would not admit him. But Martin smiled at them as he walked past the window. He was known to all the officials and was readily admitted. After he had fed the prisoners, Martin promised to pray for them and went back to the convent happy because one old hat had accomplished so much.

Newcomers to Lima often stopped to stare at Martin and the procession of stray animals and homeless children who followed him about the city. Incredible as it seems, many Spaniards abandoned their families when they moved on to other countries of the New World where rumor had it that greater riches were still to be found. As the years passed, Lima was over-run with orphans and foundlings. The more children Martin provided for, the more seemed

to appear when he gave out food the next
time. He went to the civil authorities, but they
admitted that they could not provide for so
many orphans.

When Martin had exhausted all of his re-
sources, he began praying for guidance in the
matter of caring for Lima's homeless children.
After many days of fasting and prayer, he
realized that the only solution was the building
of a school and orphanage. Martin knew he
would have to go to the public for money to
finance the orphanage, but he also knew how
to prick the consciences of the rich. He visited
every influential or wealthy person he knew,
and so touched their hearts with his stories of
the children of the streets that they agreed on
the need for an orphanage and school.

One of God's special blessings to Martin
had been the continuing friendship of Don
Mateo Pastor and his wife, Doña Francisca,
who had been cured by touching Martin's
habit. When the chemist and his wife heard
about the proposed school and orphanage, they
immediately donated two hundred thousand
pesos. The Viceroy and the Archbishop also
lent their support and sanction. Few, if any, of
the merchants were able to withstand Martin's
pleas for the children.

Within a few years Martin's dream became
a reality. *Colegio de la Santa Cruz,* the School
of the Holy Cross, opened its door to children
of all races. The cause of these orphaned
children of Lima had become so popular that
Martin might have enlisted the aid of enough
volunteers to staff the institution. Instead, he
secured the services of the best teachers, nurses,
doctors and guardians that could be found in
all Peru. He paid these people good wages but
demanded that they maintain the highest possible standards at the school. Indian, Negro, mulatto and Spanish children lived as brothers and
sisters. All were tutored in the basic subjects,
but the boys were taught trades and the girls
were taught to cook, sew and keep house.

The orphanage did not detract from Brother
Martin's other charities. He had developed a
system whereby he allotted monies begged on
certain days to certain projects. Though he
would have laughed at the idea that he kept a
record of what was given him, the meager
notes he left at his death provided enough information for his brothers in religion to learn
the scope of his charities. The money collected
on Tuesdays and Wednesdays was always set
aside for the poor. Martin used whatever he
took in on Thursdays and Fridays for the re-

lief of poor clerics. The Poor Souls in Purgatory were benefited by funds Martin took in on Saturdays and Mondays, as he had Masses said for them. The Sunday collection was small, but Martin used whatever it was to buy blankets for poor Negro, Indian and Spanish women.

Brother Martin did not confine his efforts to the physical needs of the poor; he often gave spiritual instructions, particularly in the prisons. Later he would send for a priest who either baptized the prisoners or heard the confessions of those who had strayed from the Church.

Martin had just finished one of these visits one day when he decided to stop in the prison chapel. In a far corner, in the company of a guard, he recognized Juan Gonzalez, a prisoner who was to be hanged the following day. Martin was pleased that the authorities were allowing the condemned man to spend his last hours in prayer.

As Martin rose from his knees, Gonzalez called out to him, "Brother Martin! Brother Martin!"

"God bless you, Juan Gonzalez," Martin said softly as he knelt beside the troubled man.

"Oh, Brother Martin"—the prisoner grabbed

Martin's hand—"promise me that you will pray that I may receive the strength and courage to die a true Christian."

"I shall be happy to pray for you," Martin promised, and the condemned man was smiling when the guard led him back to his cell.

All the way back to the convent Martin thought about Juan Gonzalez's request. The man had not asked him to pray that his life be spared; he had asked only for the strength and courage to die as a true Christian. This was not the request of an unrepentant man. Convinced that Juan should be pardoned, Martin had settled on a course of action by the time he reached the convent—but he would have to work fast. He first sent a servant to the jail to tell Juan Gonzalez that he was not to despair of his life. Then he went to the chapel to beg God's help in his latest adventure.

When the servant reached the jail, the warden refused to open the door for him.

"But Brother Martin sent me," the man argued. "I have an important message for Juan Gonzalez."

At Martin's name the warden opened the door and showed the servant to Juan's cell.

When the doomed man received Martin's message, he began to weep.

"My prayers are answered," Juan cried. "Brother Martin says I will not have to die, and everybody knows that the Viceroy is one of his best friends. Thank Brother Martin!" he said over and over. When the servant left, the other prisoners were already talking about the good fortune of Juan Gonzalez.

The next morning, Juan's high hopes were destroyed when the warden told him to prepare for the gallows.

"Your holy friend must have forgotten to pray for you," one of the prisoners taunted, but most of them were sad because Brother Martin had also promised to pray for them, and they began to wonder if he would forget them, too.

Juan did not give up hope. He continued to pray silently. Every time he heard a footstep, he expected to see Brother Martin rushing down the corridor to his cell. But no one came except the warden, and then the jailer who was to lead Juan through the streets of Lima to the gallows which stood in the square outside the Viceroy's palace. Even as Juan was following the jailer to the square, he looked anxiously among the crowds of people who had gathered to see him walk to his death. He refused to believe that Brother Martin had forsaken him, and it was only when he stood at the foot of the gallows that he became resigned to his fate. Then he squared his shoulders and prayed for strength to walk up the steps.

Suddenly there was a stir among the people. Juan's back was turned, but he heard the crowd give a loud gasp, then a cheer. He turned to see the Countess of Chinchon, wife of the Viceroy, standing on the balcony of the palace. Her hand was raised, a signal that the execution was to be stayed. To the amazement of the crowd, she announced that Juan Gonzalez was to receive full pardon in the name of the Count of Chinchon, Viceroy of Peru.

Juan Gonzalez was so happy that he wanted to run immediately to the convent to thank Martin. The warden restrained him. "Brother Martin has sent you a package," he said. "He gave instructions that you were to get it when you came back from the gallows. At that time nobody understood what he meant; we thought it didn't matter much."

When Juan returned to the jail, he opened the package and found a new shirt, a pair of trousers, and thirty pesos—all that he needed to make a new start in life.

Sometimes, in his dealings with prisoners, Martin had to play the role of Sherlock Holmes. This was the case when all Lima was grieving over damaging charges which had been made against a well-known priest, the outcome of a plot so cleverly planned and carried out that the most able judges had been deceived. But Martin followed one lead after another, gathering evidence with which he hoped to clear the good name of the priest. In spite of threatening notes from the instigator of the plot, Martin did not rest until he had collected enough evidence to go to the authorities and bring about not only the release of the priest but the arrest of the real culprit.

CHAPTER *8*

All God's Creatures

Around the year 1619, when Brother Martin was forty years old, a seven-year-old boy, Juan de Guarnido, came to live at the convent. The lad attached himself to Brother Martin and after a while he was like Martin's shadow. Little Juan, or Juanito, as he was called, together with a dog and a cat, comprised Martin's intimate "family" at Holy Rosary. He raised the dog and cat in the convent cellar, where these two natural enemies ate out of the same plate.

One of the most charming stories told about Martin concerns a mouse who peeped out of a hole one day as Martin and Juanito were watching the animals eat. When he saw the dog and cat, the mouse scampered away, even though Martin had thrown him a few crumbs. Touched by the tiny creature's fright, Martin stooped down near the hole. "Little Brother Mouse, I think you must be hungry. Come out and eat," he cajoled, "for no harm will come to you."

The mouse peeped out of the hole again. Martin smiled and bade the dog and cat move closer together so the mouse might share their food. Juanito watched, astonished, to see what would happen, though Martin was acting as if this were an everyday occurrence. The mouse darted back into his hole, then came out again and ran over to the plate and helped the dog and cat finish the meal. Martin talked softly to the animals as they ate, but the boy kept his distance. The next day the mouse joined them for another meal, and after that Juanito always prepared enough for the three.

But everyone at Holy Rosary did not share

Martin's fondness for "Little Brother Mouse."
An old man who had been nursed back to
health by Brother Martin and who had continued to live at the convent complained one
day that mice were eating his stockings. Martin
paid little attention to the complaints until the
man said: "I am going to set traps all over the
convent and get rid of these mice."

"If you had not dropped crumbs around or
left your stockings where the mice could find
them," Martin reminded him, "they would not
have bothered you. It would be cruel for you
to harm the little creatures."

The old man sulked, but Martin hoped he
would be more careful and that the mice would
not eat his stockings.

This was only the beginning. One by one,
Brothers from all over the convent began to
tell Martin about the damage the mice were
doing. They had eaten holes in the infirmary
and refectory linens. Even the treasured altar
cloths were beginning to show signs of damage.
"If you had not started feeding that mouse
who eats with your dog and cat in the cellar,"
scolded the sacristan, "this would not have
happened."

Martin knew that he would have to stop his
little friends from eating the cloths which

adorned God's altar. "I will find a way to stop it," he promised.

"I have already taken steps to stop it, Brother Martin," the sacristan declared. "I have set traps."

Martin hurried to the sacristy, and his heart ached to see that already one of the little creatures had fallen into a trap. As he raised the bar on the trap, Martin said, "Go along, little brother, and tell your companions not to do any more harm. All of you must vacate this monastery and go back into the garden, where I will bring you food each day."

All of the mice and even some rats crawled out of their holes and trooped to an old shed in the garden. Little Brother Mouse, who lived in the cellar and ate with the dog and cat, joined the others in the shed. Each day Martin carried food out to them, always reminding them that they were never to enter the convent.

Martin's love for God's creatures extended to larger animals as well. One vacation time, when Martin's old teacher, Dr. de Rivero, was visiting Holy Rosary, some bulls and calves were brought to the convent so that the young novices might play with them during recreation periods. One day, when Martin seemed distressed, Dr. de Rivero asked what was wrong.

"I have just learned that the animals that were brought here to provide recreation for the novices have been without food or water for four days," Martin declared.

The doctor later saw Martin place several jugs of water outside the doors leading to the novitiate and the enclosure where the bulls were kept, but he paid little attention, for he knew that the doors were locked. Martin went back and forth between the convent stables and the novitiate, his arms filled with hay, mumbling about human beings who would allow animals to go without food just because the hungry bull was the bull who provided the most sport. He placed the hay outside the locked novitiate doors, beside the water.

That night, when all of the Dominicans were supposed to be asleep, Father Diego de la Fuente, who had been late finishing his work in the novitiate, happened to be looking out of the window. He saw Martin feeding the hunger-crazed animals, speaking softly to them while he offered the hay. Father de la Fuente was tempted to call out to Martin, but the animals looked so wild that he was afraid his cry would startle them and they might trample

Martin. So he watched in silence as Martin talked to the bulls until their mood changed and they rubbed against him as if trying to kiss his habit. He fed them according to their age, saying: "You, brother, are older. Give the younger a chance to eat."

The next day broken pieces of the jugs which Doctor de Rivero had seen Martin place at the novitiate door were found about the same time Father de la Fuente was telling his superior what he had seen. When Doctor de Rivero added his testimony, they all went to the enclosure where the bulls were kept and found that the animals were now as gentle as lambs.

Though Martin had inherited his mother's coloring and curly hair, his features bespoke his Spanish, as well as African, blood. It could not be said that he was a handsome man, but his gentle smile gave his face a pleasant glow. When the glow was absent, Martin's companions knew that he was grieved. The day he heard that the procurator of the convent had ordered his aging dog to be turned out, it was apparent to all that Martin was greatly disturbed.

The dog had served his master for eighteen years, but the procurator had no further need of such a feeble dog and had told his servant to put him outside the convent gate so that he might wander away. But the faithful dog would not leave and always found a way to return to his master's cell. Finally, the procurator had the decrepit animal taken a distance from the convent and put to death. When Martin heard that the dog had been killed, he sent Juanito to fetch the body and ordered it put in his cell.

Martin went to the procurator's office. "My Father," he asked, "why did you order them to kill that animal? Is that the reward you give your dog who has served you so many years?" Before the astonished priest could answer, Brother Martin hurried back to his own cell.

The next day one of the brothers who had been concerned with the matter was startled to see the dog leaving Martin's cell with his rescuer. The news was circulated that Martin had restored the dog to life. A group of his companions found him in the kitchen feeding the animal, who looked much healthier than when he had been sent away.

"Now you be sure not to return to your ungrateful master's service," Martin was heard to tell the dog, "for you have experienced only too clearly how little your long years of faithfulness have been appreciated."

The dog followed Martin around for years afterward, but fled whenever his former master approached.

The feathered animals, too, were Martin's friends. Sometimes, when he walked through the garden with Juanito, birds would light on his shoulder. As he talked to them, Martin would take a piece of bread from the cuff of his sleeve and feed them.

He was praying in the garden of the monastery the day a great hawk, who had been wounded in the leg by a sportsman, fell at his feet with a wild cry. The enraged bird was struggling in pain. Juanito, who had heard the bird's cry, ran to see what had happened and begged Martin not to touch the bird, reminding him of the hawk's reputation as a bird of prey.

Martin smiled at Juanito's fears. "Be still," he told the big bird. "You are among friends."

The boy's eyes widened in wonder as the ferocious hawk became like a gentle dove. Martin sent Juanito to the infirmary for bandages and medicine. Then he examined the bird's wounded leg, put a healing salve on the hole left by the bullet, and bound it tightly.

Martin cared for the bird as if he had been a child. When he was too busy to get to the garden, he sent Juanito to feed him or attend to his leg. A few days later the huge bird spread his wings and flew away.

The hawk did not forget his friend, however, and one day when Martin was in the garden with Juanito, the bird came back and greeted him affectionately. After that, Juanito and the other children became accustomed to seeing the hawk swoop down out of the sky and light on the shoulder of Brother Martin, friend of all God's creatures.

CHAPTER **9**

Olive Trees and Dowries

By the time Martin reached his mid-fifties, his friends marveled that he showed few signs of the ceaseless toil with which he had filled the years. He was seldom known to sleep, except in ecstasy, and none could recall having seen him eat meat. His supply of strength appeared as boundless as his gifts of grace.

One evening after Martin had been to Lima

on some charitable errand, he made a short-cut to the convent by going through the Dominican cemetery. He heard a sound, much like a child crying, but told himself that no child would be in a cemetery at that hour. He had almost reached the gate when he heard the noise again and decided to investigate. As he walked among the tombstones, he saw a shadow which turned out to be a boy.

"What is wrong, my son?" Martin asked, bending down to look into the little face. "Why are you here instead of at home."

"I have no home," the child blurted, and he burst into tears again. Martin knelt beside the boy, wiped his tear-stained face, and gently questioned him until he learned that the child's name was Juan Vasquez de la Parra. His father had come to the New World in the service of the king but had later been recalled to Spain, leaving the child behind. When months passed without news or money from the father, the people with whom the father left his son had evidently abandoned the child.

"Come with me," Martin told the boy after he heard his story. "You will feel better after a bath and a good meal." This seven-year-old reminded Martin of Juanito, who was now grown up and had left the convent. Martin bathed the child, fed him, and put him to sleep on the cot in the closet adjoining his cell where Juanito had once slept. To avoid confusion, Martin called the lad Juancho, an affectionate name for Juan. He followed Martin around and soon learned to be helpful in many ways.

Juancho had not been living at the convent very long when the city was shaken by a terrible earthquake. Martin kept much of the clothing and the money he collected for the poor in the place where Juancho slept. The noise of the coins spilling on the floor awakened the boy, and then he was almost smothered by clothing and blankets falling on his cot. He got himself free and ran to Brother Martin's cell, but when he opened the door, he put his hand over his mouth to stifle a scream. Martin was lying on the floor, his arms outstretched so that his body formed a cross. There was a brick in his mouth.

Thinking that Brother Martin had been killed by the vibrations, Juancho ran to the cell of one of the priests and told him what had happened. The priest surmised that Martin had fallen into one of his ecstasies while praying that the city of Lima be spared further damage. "Be quiet, son," he said. "Brother Martin is neither dead nor is he going to die. You are fortunate to have witnessed what so many would be happy to see. Come with me and and sleep in my cell."

When he awoke the next morning, Juancho was surprised to learn that it was already eight o'clock, and today was Saturday, the day he always helped Martin give out food and clothing to the poor! Worse yet, Juancho remembered that he had locked Brother Martin's cell from the outside, to make sure that no one disturbed him during the night. Surely Brother Martin would be angry with him for oversleeping. As Juancho ran down a corridor to unlock the cell, he was astonished to come face to face with Brother Martin himself. Before Juancho could speak, Martin began to scold him for having told what he had seen the night before.

"Take care that you never mention such things again," Martin insisted, and then told Juancho to get the clothing which they were to take to the poor.

Juancho tried to follow Martin's wishes and for a while he told nobody about many of the strange and wonderful things which happened when he was with Brother Martin. But Juancho's confessor and several of the priests told the boy that he did not have the right to keep such things secret. These marvels were the work of God, and Juancho was to be an important link in the chain of events which would one day spread the news of Martin's sanctity throughout the world.

Juancho was happy in his new life, though there was much which he did not understand. But gradually he learned to carry out instructions first and ask their meaning afterward. If they were on a journey and Brother Martin told him to hurry his steps, Juancho knew that his adopted father had a reason; someone ahead must be in need of him. If Juancho looked up at gray skies and said that it was going to rain, and Martin said that it was not, Juancho accepted Martin's word.

Brother Martin was pleased with the boy's progress and gave him tasks which showed his trust. After several months had passed, Juancho like many others in and around Lima, was calling Martin, "Father."

On the Feast of Pentecost Juancho always had a special chore. Martin would buy two shirts of coarse cloth, one for himself and the other for Brother John Masias. He would then remove the hairshirt he had been wearing and bury it under a lemon tree just outside the infirmary door. Then Juancho would follow

Martin to the Convent of St. Mary Magdalen, where he visited Brother John. The two friends would retire to a banana garden on the convent property, place a picture of Our Lord on the limb of a tree, and spend the entire day in prayer and penance.

From time to time Juancho would go to the garden to see if Martin needed him. Often the face and any other exposed part of Martin's body was covered with mosquitoes. One night, after a day spent in the garden, Martin asked Juancho to apply a salve to the bites on his shoulders. The boy asked why he stayed in the garden since he knew that mosquitoes would bite him.

"They, too, are God's creatures," Martin said, laughing, "and must have food. This is a small bit of suffering in comparison to what He suffered for us."

After a few years Juancho stopped worrying about Martin's mosquito bites. At certain times of the year he made sure there was a supply of salve in the closet off Martin's cell where he slept.

It was high noon in the month of July the day Martin told Juancho that they were to go to the Amanceas Valley to plant chamomile,

one of the herbs Martin used in the infirmary.
After reaching their destination, Juancho and
Martin spent all afternoon setting out plants.
Juancho was hungry, tired, and anxious to get
back to the convent. As they walked a short
distance of what Juancho thought was their
return journey, Martin told him they would
first have to go to a village called Lurigancho.
After an hour or so on the road, Juancho
began to complain of thirst, but Martin showed
no signs of concern. Juancho trudged along
until it became obvious that he could not go
much farther.

"*Now* you will have water," Martin told the
boy, and Juancho saw an Indian, who had a
canteen of water slung over his shoulder, ap-
proaching them.

"I'm hungry, too," Juancho complained after
the Indian had shared his water with the boy.

"Will you please give this boy a piece of
bread," Martin asked the Indian, "since you so
kindly gave him water?"

"Father," the Indian replied, "I am at your
service," and the man handed Juancho a piece
of bread before he went on his way.

Even as the boy nibbled at the bread, Martin
urged him to hurry. Soon they reached Lurigancho, and Juancho thought they would stop

and rest a while. But Martin walked on and on until they came to a farm owned by a Spaniard. As soon as they set foot upon the property, a tall Negro came to meet them.

"Is there anyone sick in there?" Martin pointed toward the servants' quarters.

"Yes," the Negro answered in surprise. "My wife is very sick and today she received Extreme Unction."

Martin and Juancho followed the man to his hut where his wife lay ill.

When she asked how Martin had learned of her illness, he replied, "Daughter, do not be discouraged. With the help of God you will be all right."

Then he told the husband to go to a near-by canal, catch three toads, put them in a pot and cook them, without letting any of the steam escape.

The man did as he was told. Martin ground the steamed toads into a powder, and put it into an old cloth which he fastened around the woman's waist.

"Daughter," he told her, "I am applying a remedy, and may God cure you completely. Tomorrow morning I will send Juancho to find out what kind of night you had. He will bring some candles with him. God willing, you can rest comfortably."

The next morning Martin sent Juancho back to Lurigancho with ten candles and four loaves of bread. He was told to find out how the sick woman was. When Juancho reached the farm, he was met by the owner, who asked him where he was going.

"Sir, I have here some bread and candles which Brother Martin de Porres has sent to a sick woman who lives on this farm," replied Juancho.

"The one who after God has saved the life of my servant, Margarita?" asked the owner. "Come, let us go together to see her."

Juancho was surprised to find Margarita sitting up in a chair. "What kind of night did you have, Margarita?" asked the owner. "After the remedies that Brother Martin gave me, master," she replied, "I slept very well the night through. May God reward him."

The grateful owner took Juancho to his house and fed him, then insisted that he should take a mule back to the convent as a gift to Martin.

Not long after they had visited Margarita, Brother Martin told Juancho that they were going to return to the valley where they had planted the herbs. On the way home, they passed an orchard which did not seem to belong to anyone. Martin stopped and said, "I want to get a branch of a fig tree and plant it on a certain hill." He cut a branch about as thick as his wrist. When they reached a small hill on the outskirts of town, Martin planted the switch which he had cut from the fig tree.

About two weeks later Martin and Juancho returned to the spot. The branch which had been put into the ground so recently was now a tree in bud. "Thanks be to God!" Martin said. "Two or three years from now it will have figs on it and the poor people who pass this way can stop and eat of its fruit."

Brother Martin's success with trees was soon demonstrated to Juancho on a much broader scale. The boy had thought they were preparing for a routine journey when Martin gave him a large supply of graham bread which he had carefully wrapped. Juancho wondered what they would do with so much bread. Finally he asked Martin, and was told that they were going to Limatambo to perform a service to God which would require them to be absent for two months.

"What will we do that will take us so long?" Juancho asked.

"Father Francisco is pruning the olive grove," Martin said, "and you and I are going to cut some slips from the trees. We shall plant a new olive grove which will extend from the Royal Highway to the Mill. It will provide food and a place of recreation for the novices during their probation. The present olive grove is very old and this new one will take its place. Thirty years from now, when it is fully grown and these young men are fully matured, they will say, 'May God bless the man who planted this grove!'"

As Martin and Juancho walked along, they met many homeless boys to whom they gave graham bread. "One day," Martin told each of them, "you will help me work."

When Martin and Juancho reached the plantation, they went to the olive grove where Father Francisco was pruning the trees, just as Martin had said. Martin asked Father Francisco to put aside some slips, explaining that he had decided to plant a new grove which would extend from the Royal Highway to the Mill.

The priest smiled at Martin and asked him how he proposed to set out such a large number of slips.

"Don't worry," Martin replied, "the Providence of God is all-powerful. The boys in the house will prepare the slips. Will you please give me two servants and four mules to carry them for planting?"

The next day Juancho watched Martin as he divided the slips he had been given into four piles, one for each mule. After the servants had loaded the packs on the animals, the little procession set out for the site Martin had chosen. Juancho did not pay much attention to the first boys who joined them on the road. After a while, as the number swelled, he noticed that all of the faces seemed familiar. They were the boys to whom Martin had given the graham bread.

Martin showed the boys and the servants how to dig the holes into which he would put the slips. He insisted that each should be a little less than a yard deep and a quarter of a yard wide. At the end of the first day, Juancho counted ninety holes already dug. After a week there were enough to receive all the slips. Juancho thought there were more holes than slips, but he waited to see what would happen.

That Saturday, Martin arose thanking God for letting him see the light of the day upon which his planting would begin. He told Juancho and the servants that one of the four piles could be planted each week. They did not think they could work so fast, but Martin insisted that it would be possible. The little crew worked very hard, but Juancho and the boys said that two slips seemed to appear in the place of each one they put in the ground. At noon Martin would spread a lunch for his workers and allow them a few minutes of rest. In spite of the manner in which the slips seemed to multiply, at the end of the week every slip from the first pile had been set in the ground.

The following Monday Martin began watering the plants. By the third day of watering all of them had budded. The sight of blossoms on the slips which had only been planted a few days before so encouraged the planters that they worked doubly hard. In two weeks' time they set out seven hundred olive branches, and by the end of the month these plants extended from the Royal Highway to the Mill.

Martin and Juancho remained in Limatambo for some time before they returned to Lima. The very next time they visited the plantation, Martin took Juancho past the new olive grove and the boy saw green olives on the saplings. For the rest of his life, Juancho thrilled each time he walked past "Brother Martin's olive grove," as the natives called the garden which

extended from the Royal Highway to the Mill.
The grove provided food for the novices, as
well as for the poor and their children, who
knew that they were welcome to the fruit from
the trees Brother Martin had planted.

Martin's heart always ached when he saw the
children of the poor deprived of necessities
and healthy pleasures. For a long time he had
grieved over the many lovely young girls he
knew who wanted to join a religious community or get married but could do neither because they did not have money or property
for a dowry.

With the help of one or two friends, Martin
was able to provide modest dowries for the
girls who lived at the orphanage he had
founded. When they were ready to leave the
institution, the money was handed over to
them. Yet Martin knew there were so many
other poor girls in Lima who faced the future
without any hope because of the custom which
made it necessary for a girl to bring a sum of
money to her husband or the religious order
she entered.

Martin always remembered his troubles about
Juana's dowry many years before—so many
years before, in fact, that now Juana's daughter, Catalina, was ready to be married. Her

suitor, Melchior, was a good, hard-working young man and a desirable husband, but Catalina's parents were unable to provide her with a dowry. Martin was sad and wished that he could help his niece.

He had not long to worry, however, for as soon as word got around that Brother Martin's niece needed a dowry, all Lima wanted to help. Don Juan de Figueroa, who had been cured of his throat ailment, immediately gave a gift and insisted on being a witness to the publication of the marriage banns. The Archbishop also gave a gift and offered to make all the wedding arrangements himself. Don Juan then invited Martin to his warehouse to choose fine linens and a beautiful dress of Castilian cloth for Catalina.

As soon as Martin and Don Juan were seen on the street, other merchants left their shops to congratulate Martin and press gifts upon him. Their generosity overwhelmed him, and after Catalina's happy wedding day he began to think about the other poor girls of Lima who needed dowries. Would not the rich merchants be as generous to these poor girls?

Martin first approached his old friend, Don Mateo, who readily agreed to furnish dowries for twenty-seven girls—but he made a stipulation which cast Martin in a role he had never dreamed of. Don Mateo would give the dowries only if Brother Martin would agree to find husbands for the marriageable girls.

But finding the first twenty-seven husbands was not so easy a job as one would think. Martin and Juancho had to find out all there was to know about every single man in Lima. Merchants helped them by pointing out likely young men in the market place, sometimes travelers who were passing through Lima. When Juancho could not strike up a conversation with a young man, he would run to the convent to get Martin to talk to him and see if he would make a good husband. Neither Martin nor Juancho rested until they had found good husbands for all twenty-seven girls. This is why Martin has become known as a patron of lovers and affairs of the heart.

CHAPTER *10*

Juancho

It was not unusual for Juancho to come upon Martin suspended in air as he prayed before the altar or knelt before the crucifix in his cell. When he gazed on the crucifix Martin's body seemed to be drawn toward it, regardless of the distance between. Though Martin's ecstasies were not unusual, they never ceased to fill Juancho with awe. Sometimes, when Martin remained in this state longer than Juancho expected, the boy became fearful, but the friars comforted him, saying that Martin would not leave him, even to go to Our Lord, without a word of parting. The Dominicans were grateful to Juancho, for he could tell them many of the wonders which Martin performed and which they would not otherwise hear of. Moreover, Juancho was now fifteen years of age and was proving to be a joy to Martin in his older years.

Martin had taught Juancho the barber's trade and sometimes let the boy help him. One day, as Juancho was handling the shears very well and Martin was looking on proudly, the Viceroy came by to leave his monthly gift of money which Martin then distributed to the poor. Martin told the Viceroy that Juancho had mastered the barber's trade very well and would be soon prepared to go out into the world and make a living for himself. Juancho thought it odd that Martin would take up the time of so important a person as the Viceroy with a discussion of the future of a homeless boy. Then he remembered that in the past few months Martin had reminded him several times that his trade would enable him to make his way in the world "when the time comes."

"Perhaps he is displeased with me," Juancho thought, as his customer left and he began to sweep the floor.

Martin and the Viceroy were talking in low tones. When Martin saw that Juancho had finished sweeping, he asked the boy to gather up the money, which the Viceroy had placed on a table, and take it to the closet off his cell. As Juancho efficiently stacked the money into neat piles, the Viceroy watched approvingly and then said, "This boy should be enlisted as a soldier in the king's service. We would treat him well."

Martin smiled and nodded in agreement. He seemed so pleased with the suggestion that Juancho began to wonder why his adopted father would seem so pleased at the thought of his going away.

For the next few weeks Juancho was miserable. He had not felt so alone in the world since the night Martin had found him in the cemetery. From time to time, Martin complimented him on a chore or an errand well performed and said that he was pleased with his progress. Each compliment made Juancho a little more miserable. He wished desperately that he could summon courage enough to run away from the convent or ask Martin why he wished to be rid of him.

When the Viceroy made his next monthly visit, Martin again called Juancho to put the money away. This time Juancho's hands trembled nervously as he stacked the coins. The Viceroy repeated what he had said before about Juancho's joining the army, and Juancho nearly dropped the money bag when Martin replied that the boy would surely enlist in the army if that was His Excellency's wish, but a commission should be issued for Juancho in the king's name.

Juancho was even more bewildered when the Viceroy ordered him to call his servant, who immediately wrote out the commission. The boy listened as Martin spoke highly of his qualifications to the Viceroy.

"But, Father—" was as far as Juancho ever got with his objections to being sent away to the army, for each time he tried to speak, Martin told him that what was being done was for the best.

That night Juancho was sitting on his bed, wondering why he was being sent away, when Martin came in. "Tomorrow morning," Martin said, "you will have to go to Callao without fail. Present yourself to the regiment of the field marshal with this memorandum and decree in order that they may place you, which they will do immediately."

"Father"—Juancho bit his lip so that the hurt would keep back the tears—"why are you sending me away?"

"I am not sending you away, my son. The time has come when you must make your way in the world. Everything is for the best. You will see me more often than you think."

Martin had said everything was for the best and Juancho knew that his adopted father had wisdom which had been granted very few men. So he resigned himself to what seemed to be his fate.

In September, 1637, Martin said *adios* to the boy who had been a son to him, and Juancho set out for Callao, trying hard to hide his sadness. Martin kept smiling and telling him that this was not a final good-by. On the road to Callao, Juancho met a well-known soldier, Don Juan de Lusa, who asked where the boy was going. Juancho explained that he was going to enlist in the army and added that, at the request of Brother Martin, the Viceroy had given him a commission.

"Come with me to my regiment," De Lusa said, "for I shall be glad to have you. In this way I, too, can please that servant of God, Brother Martin."

De Lusa was a pleasant man, and in his company Juancho forgot some of the sadness which had marked the first part of his journey. When they reached Callao, De Lusa took him to the royal barracks where he was to submit his credentials and begin the business of becoming a soldier in the king's army. Afterwards, as Juancho left the barracks to take a walk, he heard someone call his name. It was Brother Martin.

Embracing the boy, Martin said, "Now, my son, you have a master to serve."

Don Juan de Lusa saw Martin and ran out to speak with him. After exchanging greetings with the lieutenant, Martin told him what a faithful assistant and dutiful son Juancho had been to him. "Lieutenant," he said, "for the love of God, please be kind to this boy, for he is not used to military service as are others whom you have here."

"Everything will be done for him, Father, according to your wishes," the soldier assured Martin, and the three walked as far as the Plaza of St. Augustine.

De Lusa invited Martin to have dinner with

him, but Martin explained that he was taking a mule back to the convent and did not want to keep the poor animal standing in the sun too long. When the soldier left them, Martin talked to Juancho about his new obligations and told the boy that he wanted him to remain in the king's service.

There was a worried expression on Juancho's face as he listened to what Martin said. He had heard that soldiers were paid every eight months and that they had to provide their own food.

"How will I eat," the boy asked, "for I have no money?"

"You will have no cause for worry." Martin gave Juancho five pesos, which he took from the pocket of his habit. "Whenever you are without money, find your way to the convent and ask for Father Alonso. I will instruct him to supply your needs."

Juancho did not have much of a chance to get homesick, for Martin showed up at the barracks in Callao often during the early days of his service. He was sympathetic and encouraging, and as the months passed Juancho became accustomed to the military life. Whenever he had cause to go to the convent and appeal to Father Alonso, his needs were always supplied. De Lusa, too, was anxious to please Martin and consequently was very kind to Juancho.

After two years, Juancho was appointed company barber and was then offered an opportunity to go with part of the regiment to Spain. De Lusa would buy all the supplies Juancho would need to set up a barber shop on board ship. Juancho was thrilled at the thought of returning to his native land, where he might locate relatives and learn what had happened to his father. At the same time he was worried because he had not consulted Martin. As he was making preparations to go to Lima, Martin appeared outside the barracks.

"I am grieved at the thought of your leaving the country," Martin said before Juancho could speak. "If you will stay, I would be happy to set up a barber shop for you in Lima. All of my friends would come to you."

Juancho explained that he was going only to seek another promotion and to look for his father. "There will be time enough for the shop when I return," he said.

Martin embraced the young soldier. "*Adios*, Juancho. We shall not meet again in this world.

And if we ever see each other again," he added, "you will doubt it."

Juancho sailed away to a bright future and many years were to pass before he understood Martin's words.

CHAPTER 11

Brother Martin's New Habit

Martin's gift of prophecy had been used through the years to guide and benefit his Brothers and friends. Now at last, as he neared the age of sixty, he made an important prophecy concerning himself. Don Juan de Figueroa had been at odds with the Viceroy over an administrative matter but, as Martin had predicted, the matter was resolved in favor of Don Juan.

Martin had also predicted, however, that misfortune would befall Don Juan. And so it happened. His friends turned against him, he had financial reverses, and he became seriously ill. Thinking he had reached his final hours, De Figueroa sent one of his servants for Martin.

"Please promise to pray for me when I am in my last agony," he begged as soon as Martin came into the room. "Ask God to give me resignation to His holy will."

"I shall die before you," Brother Martin said, smiling, "so you must pray for me. But rest assured I shall not forget you."

Don Juan recovered and later went to the Convent of the Holy Rosary to visit Brother Martin. After talking of many things, De Figueroa confided that he was thinking of having a shrine built at the Church of Our Lady of Mercy, where he might also build a vault and tomb for himself.

Martin complimented his friend on his good intention. "Build the shrine," he said, "but do not reserve a tomb there. It is here"—and Martin pointed to the floor of his own cell where they were sitting—"that they are going to bury both of us."

Meanwhile the Archbishop of Mexico, who had long been a friend of Martin's, was visiting the convent when he was stricken with pneumonia. The most eminent doctors in the city were called in, but all hope for his life was abandoned.

Father Cypriano de Medina, the Archbishop's nephew—that same Cypriano who, as an ugly seminarian, had been transformed by Martin's prayers—was also at the convent. When he learned of his uncle's serious condition, he asked why no one had sent for Brother Martin. He set out immediately to look for him, but Martin was not to be found.

The Archbishop continued to grow weaker and for three long hours the friars felt sure they were watching his death struggle. He begged for Martin and said that he could not understand why his old friend would forsake him.

When the doctors said that death was only minutes away, Father de Medina went to the chapel to pray. Suddenly he remembered that Martin usually came at the exact moment when the need for him was greatest. He also remembered that Martin's most cherished vow was obedience. From the pew where he knelt, he could see Father Provincial in the sacristy. "If the Provincial orders Brother Martin to appear," thought Cypriano, "he will."

He hurried to the sacristy and told Father Provincial about his plan.

"Very well," agreed the Provincial. Then he called out, "Brother Martin, as your superior, I command you in the name of holy obedience to appear at once!"

As the sound of the last word died away, Martin entered the door of the sacristy. He was smiling, as usual, and the Provincial did not question him. "Brother Martin," he said, "surely you must know that your good friend, Don Feliciano, is seriously ill. Go to his room and obey him as you would a superior."

As soon as the Archbishop saw Martin, he chided him for not having visited him earlier and asked him to place his hand on the side where the pain was greatest. Martin shrank from making a show of anything which would make him appear to be a wonder-worker, but he remembered that Father Provincial had ordered him to be obedient to the Archbishop.

"Your Excellency," Martin began, "how can you make such a request of a lowly Brother?"

"Dear Brother Martin, your Provincial ordered you to obey me, didn't he?" the sick man asked in a voice that was little more than a whisper. "Therefore put your hand on this side where I suffer so much pain. I command you to do this in the name of holy obedience."

Martin made the sign of the cross and placed his hand on the side of the Archbishop. Suddenly all eyes in the room moved anxiously in the direction of the sickbed.

"It is better," the Archbishop gasped. "It is much better!" And he went into a deep sleep.

The doctors stepped forward, examined the patient and, after consultation agreed that the fever had abated. It was also obvious that the pain had subsided or the Archbishop would not have slept so soundly. Martin slipped quietly out of the room.

That evening the Archbishop's recovery was so complete that his thoughts were of home, and he began making plans for the return voyage. He was so grateful that he asked the Provincial to allow him to take Brother Martin back to Mexico where he would be a part of the Archbishop's official family. The Provincial was reluctant but finally agreed.

Throughout the convent small groups gathered to discuss Brother Martin's good fortune.

The friars were sure it would only be a short time before Brother Martin would be enjoying a life of ease in the Archbishop's palace. Perhaps he might even become a priest—or a bishop! The friars were even more surprised when Martin appeared the next day in a new habit. Usually he wore a habit until it was ragged.

When one of them commented on it, Martin replied quietly, "This is the habit in which they will bury me."

Shortly before the Archbishop was to leave Lima, Brother Martin was stricken with a fever. Though he continued to work in the infirmary and insisted upon distributing money, food and clothing to the poor, it was plain to see that he was a sick man. After a few days he was so weak he could do nothing but rest upon the hard boards which had served as his bed for so long. His condition grew worse, but he refused all help until he was ordered to allow the friars to care for him. Then the Provincial sent for Dr. Francisco Navarro.

When the doctor had examined Brother Martin, he knew that his patient was in the throes of no ordinary illness. As he sat thinking of what might be the most effective remedy, Martin shook his head and sighed.

"It is useless," he told the doctor, "useless!"

Dr. Navarro gave Martin a gentle pat on his careworn hand, just as he would have done with any patient whom he wished to reassure. Then he ordered a Brother to kill some fowls and make a poultice from their blood, since this was a remedy which was supposed to reduce fevers and one which Brother Martin himself used.

Martin begged Dr. Navarro not to bother. "It will be useless," he said softly. "This is a fever which no poultice can cure. I have told you that my time has come. And why should the lives of the fowls be sacrificed needlessly?"

News spread throughout Lima that Martin had prophesied his death and had then been stricken. People began coming to the convent, begging to see him in the hope of asking one last favor. The crowd reached such proportions that the Provincial gave strict orders that nobody from the outside was to see Martin without his permission.

The friars hovered about his bed, trying to make him comfortable, hoping he would ask some small favor of them, but Martin gave little indication that he was aware of their presence. His lips moved constantly in prayer, and though he was too weak to rise from his bed

his eyes remained fixed upon the crude char-
coal cross which he had drawn on the wall of
his cell. The priests and Brothers realized that
even in illness Brother Martin was subject to
the ecstasies which had so often overcome him
as he gazed upon the crucifix.

Notables from all over Peru began coming
to the convent, but when Martin's old friend,
the Viceroy, appeared, Martin was in the midst
of one of his ecstasies. The Prior stood outside
the door of Brother Martin's cell and announced the presence of the Viceroy, but
Martin's eyes remained fixed on the cross. Over
and over the Prior called Martin's name, but
his voice fell upon deaf ears even though he
could plainly see that Martin's lips were moving and his eyes shone with the light of an
intense love.

The Viceroy begged the Prior not to dis-
turb Brother Martin, as he waited in the corridor until the vision had passed. When the
Prior finally showed the Viceroy into Martin's
little cell, the man fell on his knees, kissed
Martin's hand, and begged him to ask the
Divine Majesty that Peru might enjoy peace
and tranquility, that Christianity might be truly
established, and that he might enjoy divine

favor in this life, which might be ended by a happy death.

The kind expression which had drawn people to Martin all of his life triumphed over the pain which racked his body. He smiled, assuring the Viceroy that he would pray for him and that his requests would be granted, and told him to trust firmly in God's goodness, to confide in the merits of Our Lord Jesus Christ, and to recommend all his endeavors to the Mother of God.

After escorting the Viceroy to the gate of the convent, the Provincial hurried back to Martin's cell.

"Brother Martin," he said, "if the vision you had was so extraordinary that you felt justified in keeping the chief representative of the Spanish crown waiting, I order you to reveal it to me."

Martin sighed deeply before he spoke. "Near the altar where the Blessed Sacrament, which will be given to me as my Viaticum, is reserved," he began, "there my patroness and special advocate, the Blessed Virgin Mary, appeared to me. With her were our holy Father, St. Dominic, St. Vincent Ferrer, and other saints and angels, too. Consequently, being honored by such heavenly and supremely distinguished visitors, I did not deem it discourteous to keep an earthly Viceroy waiting."

Martin was quiet for a while, but as the evening wore on his fever made him restless and one of the priests urged him to call on St. Dominic for assistance at the hour of death.

"Oh, I am very happy indeed, for I do not have to call on our holy Father," he said. "I have already had him here in the company of the Mother of God and her faithful spouse, St. Joseph, with St. Catherine of Alexandria, and St. Vincent Ferrer, the great preacher and wonder-worker of our glorious order."

Someone placed a crucifix in Martin's hands. One of the priests administered the last sacraments, which Martin received with surprising fervor, and then for several hours he did not speak, though he continued to kiss the hands, the feet and the side of the figure on the crucifix clasped in his hands. When one of the Brothers asked if he should call the other members of the community for prayers, Martin showed by a gesture that it was not yet time. Nevertheless it was plain that Martin's suffering had become more intense. Finally, his bed shook from the violence of a seizure. Then he was still, like one who had escaped a terrible danger, and the familiar smile returned.

One of the friars again asked if he should call the others, and this time Martin nodded.

The Archbishop of Mexico, the Provincial, the Prior, some laymen, and all his Dominican brothers gathered around Martin's bed. He begged them to forgive him for what he called his "bad example." They all joined in the prayers for the dead according to the Dominican rite. As they said the Nicene Creed, at the words, "Et homo factus est"—"and He was made man"—Martin de Porres folded his arms on his bosom, one hand still pressing the crucifix, and smiled peacefully as his soul returned to his Creator.

"Let us all learn"—the Archbishop's voice broke as he tried to speak—"from the edifying death of Brother Martin how to die well. It is a lesson which is most important and most difficult."

The provincial's secretary noted that Martin's happy death took place between the hours of eight and nine in the evening on the 3rd day of November, 1639.

When the friars began to prepare Martin's body for burial, they found his waist girded by an iron chain and the remains of the rough hairshirt which Juancho had said he always wore. On his shoulders and back were scars,

the results of the severe penances he had prac-
ticed.

The body was placed in a rough casket and
set before the high altar in the main church.
The friars had barely set down their precious
burden when Indians, Negroes and Spaniards
began streaming into the church to view the
body of the man who had been their friend.
The news of Brother Martin's death seemed to
have spread as quickly as he had often appeared
when his name was called by one in need.
The old and the infirm hobbled in alongside
civil and ecclesiastical dignitaries. The children
of the rich cried as loudly as the orphans
whose existence had depended upon Martin's
baskets of food and the coins he begged for
them.

The corpse assumed the rigidity of death,
and Father Cypriano de Medina, who had so
much faith in Martin, was disappointed to see
that nothing unusual had happened to indicate
Martin's sanctity. As the people filed past the
casket, Father Cypriano whispered, "How is
it, Brother Martin, that your body is stiff and
rigid? All these good people are waiting to
behold wonders wrought by you in order to
glorify the Lord. Ask your Master to show

His supreme power by making your body lifelike!"

Within a few minutes the fragrance of roses and lilies floated around the body of Martin as it became soft and supple. When the people smelled the fragrance, there was no way to hold them back. They pressed forward, touching the body with rosaries and crucifixes. Then they began cutting bits of the new habit which Martin had said would shroud him. They cut so much of the habit away that the friars had to reclothe the body several times.

Martin's niece, Catalina, who had been a cripple for fifteen years, was grieved because she was unable to go to the convent to see her uncle during his illness. When she heard the news of his death, she begged her neighbors to carry her to the church to see his body. They helped Catalina up the aisle of the church and waited while she knelt beside the casket, begging Martin to pray for her. As she tried to get up, Catalina's legs touched the casket. Before she or her friends realized what was happening, she stood without help and looked about in wonder.

"It's another miracle," the people whispered. "Brother Martin has cured his niece!"

Catalina's friends gathered around her and,

with tears of gratitude streaming down her cheeks, Martin's niece walked slowly from the church to which she had been brought as a cripple.

Outside, an excited man was telling what had happened to Martin's old friend, Doña Isabel Ortiz, who had been miraculously cured years before. Doña Isabel had been stricken a few days before Martin suffered his final illness. She, too, was in the death agony the day she was told that Martin was dead. Looking upon a picture of her holy friend which she had commissioned an artist to paint, Doña Isabel moaned, "Venerable Brother, you helped me while you were on earth. Through your prayers God vouchsafed to cure me when my life was despaired of. Now that you are in heaven, do not abandon me."

"She was cured," the man went on, "and even now is preparing to come here so you can see with your own eyes."

The people became so emotional after the news of these two cures that the Dominicans decided to hold a private funeral and bury Martin without delay. Though nobody outside of the order was invited, some must have learned about the plan, for the Church of the

Holy Rosary was filled when the funeral Mass was said.

The half-breed child who had been baptized by Father Antonio Polanco with so little ceremony had become so revered in his lifetime that four of the most distinguished men in the New World begged for the privilege of bearing his casket to its resting place. The Viceroy of Peru, the Archbishop of Mexico, a future bishop of Cuzco, and a judge of the royal court carried Martin de Porres's casket to the chapter room, from which it was transferred to a vault in the crypt reserved for priests.

The stories of cures spread all over Lima and into surrounding towns and villages. Wherever there was sickness, someone was sure to call on Martin or bring one of the relics which had been taken from the church during the time his body lay in state. Several other cures resulted.

As reports of miracles increased, the Dominicans began to gather information from those who had known Martin and observed some of the wonders wrought by him in God's name. They also made plans to transform Martin's cell into a shrine where he would be buried, for pilgrims were already coming to the convent to visit his tomb. Remembering the friendship between Martin and Don Juan de Figueroa, who was now governor, one of the friars suggested that Don Juan might like to contribute to the establishment of such a shrine and, if the Governor wished, he too might be buried there one day. Don Juan remembered Martin's prophecy that they would be buried together in his cell, and agreed to bear all expenses. The cell was transformed into a shrine called Christ's Chapel and the relics of Martin were transferred. Governor de Figueroa lived to be extremely old, and when he died his body was buried beside that of his friend and advisor.

CHAPTER *12*

St. Martin

By 1659 an episcopal commission held a hearing on the virtues and works of Martin de Porres. The hearing lasted for several years. Dr. Marcelo de Rivero, then a very old man, testified concerning the period when Martin had been apprenticed to him and the unusual events he had witnessed at the convent. A cousin of Martin's father attested to facts concerning his birth and parentage. Among others who told of the wonders Martin had worked were Juan de Guarnido—Martin's Juanito—and Juancho, who had returned from Spain.

It was June 23, 1663, when Juancho testified the first time. He explained to the notary that he had lived at the convent with Martin and had observed many wonderful things. His enthusiasm must have frightened the notary, who probably thought that Juancho would talk too long. In any case, he cautioned Juancho to be brief. Whenever Juancho paused or choked with emotion over some of his recollections, the notary became impatient to such an extent that Juancho's first testimony was incomplete as well as brief.

Months afterward, Juancho returned to the Convent of the Holy Rosary with a strange story. He told the friars that after giving his testimony he had returned home to his wife and children. One evening, just before the first peal of the Angelus, as he was sitting at home holding one of the children in his arms, he heard his name called twice in a distant but clear voice. He went to the door and looked outside. Two Dominican friars, whom he did not know, were walking by. Juancho thought his imagination was playing tricks and returned to his family. Soon he heard his name called again.

Juancho ran to the front door but saw no one except the same two Dominicans he had seen before. This time they turned and faced him.

One of them called him by name. "Don't you recognize me?" he asked.

Looking closely at the man who had addressed him, Juancho recognized Brother Martin.

"Dear son," said Brother Martin, "why are you so shy?"

"Shy?" Juancho asked. "In what sense, Father?"

"Declare all that you know," Martin answered, "and all that you saw during the time you were in my company."

Then Martin disappeared, looking sad. Juancho thought often about this strange happening. Convinced that he was having illusions, on several occasions he was tempted to see a doctor. Then in February, 1671, he was notified to appear at the convent to make a declaration concerning Martin's life. Father Bernardo de Medina was gathering information for the first biography of Martin de Porres. Juancho felt relieved. Now he would have another chance to tell what he had seen during Brother Martin's lifetime.

As Juancho walked past the cemetery which held so many memories for him, he met Brother Martin again, still in the company of the priest who had been with him when he appeared in front of Juancho's house. "Why haven't you paid attention to the lessons of obedience I taught you?" he scolded. "This is the second time I have had to ask you. Go now and tell all that you should reveal." And Martin disappeared before Juancho could say a word in defense of his delay.

When the Dominicans had heard Juancho's story, they called in the Apostolic Notary. Juancho then told everything he could remember about his years with Brother Martin, including the farewell at Callao when Martin had told him that they would not meet again in this world and that Juancho would not recognize him when they did meet. All was recorded by the notary.

* * *

As material was being gathered for this first book on Martin's life, Pope Clement IX permitted the institution of important steps by the

Sacred Congregation of Rites in favor of Brother Martin's cause. Documents attesting to the holiness of Martin de Porres and similar papers concerning the virtues of his friend, Brother John Masias, were sent to Rome at the same time. The boat which was carrying these papers was wrecked, however, and new copies had to be made and sent to Pope Innocent XII. It was not until April 29, 1763, during the reign of Pope Clement XIII, that the Vatican issued a decree proclaiming the heroic character of Brother Martin's life and deeds. In 1836, Pope Gregory XVI declared Martin de Porres and John Masias blessed servants of God. The first steps had been taken, but more than a century would pass before Martin would be canonized.

In 1939, three hundred years after his death, Blessed Martin de Porres was declared the patron of social justice in Peru. In the land of his birth pictures and statues of Martin came to be found in all hospitals, prisons, schools, orphanages. Many institutions have been named for him, and among the people's most cherished sacramentals are "Martin's brooms," miniature reminders of the way in which their patron dignified the most lowly labor. These tiny brooms are blessed and distributed to the people, who pray that Brother Martin will continue to sweep out sin and sweep in grace.

In the meantime, Martin's fame had begun to spread throughout the United States. In 1935, Rev. Thomas McGlynn, O.P., the sculptor-priest who was already interested in the life of Martin de Porres, was in Rome when the brother of Cardinal Pacelli, later to become Pope Pius XII, fell dangerously ill. The Cardinal requested Father McGlynn to pray to Martin for his brother. This request, relayed to the Dominicans in River Forest, Illinois, prompted the first novena to Martin in the United States on January 28, 1935. Cardinal Pacelli's brother was not cured, but the novena was the beginning of a renewed devotion which was to spread.

Letters from all over the world poured in to the Vatican begging for the canonization of Martin de Porres. Cure after cure was reported, but in the case of each cure the Church demands scientific proof of a miracle.

The American Dominicans continued to foster devotion to Martin and to work for his canonization. Father McGlynn executed a statue of Martin. Reverend Edward L. Hughes and Reverend J. C. Kearns wrote about Martin's life, and Reverend Norbert Georges became director of the Blessed Martin Guild.

In October of 1961 it was reported that the doctors of the Medical Commission of the Sacred Congregation of Rites had accepted two cures as "above the power of nature." One case was that of Dorotea Caballero Escalante, who recovered from an internal obstruction and a heart attack at the age of eighty-seven after praying to Martin de Porres. This cure took place in Asunción, Paraguay, in 1948, and was said to have been almost instantaneous. The other cure involved Antonio Cabrera Perez, four years of age, who lived in Tenerife, Canary Islands. Antonio's leg was crushed when the wall of a building collapsed in 1959. Gangrene set in and amputation appeared to be inevitable. When Martin's intercession was sought, the leg was healed instantaneously.

Even after the two cures had been accepted, the reports of the doctors had to be analyzed by the promoter of the Faith and defended by the promoter of the cause of Blessed Martin. Then their reports had to be approved by the cardinals of the Congregation of Rites. It was then that Pope John XXIII declared his willingness to canonize Martin de Porres. In mid-

April, His Holiness announced May 6, 1962, as the date for Martin's canonization.

Though they had only a month, Martin's followers from all over the world began making preparations. Pilgrimages were organized and holy goods supply houses were deluged with orders for pictures of Martin and booklets on his life.

On May 6th, an estimated 30,000 people from fifty nations representing every race crowded into St. Peter's Basilica in Rome to witness the solemn ceremony for which so many had worked and waited so long. A mere 350 of the faithful were Negro pilgrims from the United States. Hundreds came from Peru, the land of Martin's birth. One of the most jubilant groups was composed of 900 Irish pilgrims who chartered a ship to take them to Rome for the canonization.

Perhaps the most grateful pilgrim attending the canonization was Antonio Perez, the boy from the Canary Islands whose life had been saved by Martin's intercession. Father Daniel W. Cantwell, whose account of the canonization appeared in the magazine, *New City*, said of the boy: "Nothing pietistic about him, quite normal, he was annoyed by the visitors who came to his parent's apartment in Rome because the visitors kept him from watching television. In his own way the lad was also serious and profound. Over the Vatican station the Sunday night of Martin's canonization, the boy pointed out that he, a little white boy, was helped by Martin, a Negro boy, and hoped that all the boys of the world would learn from Martin."

The four-hour ceremony began at 8:30 A.M. in the medieval splendor of the Sistine Chapel when Pope John intoned the hymn to the Blessed Virgin, "Hail, Star of the Sea," and received the three lighted candles traditionally offered to the Pope as homage by the supporters of a saint's cause. The Pope was then carried from the Sistine Chapel on his portable throne through the halls of the Vatican and down the Regal Stairs to St. Peter's. In a display of colorful pageantry, hundreds of cardinals, prelates and brilliantly-uniformed court officials preceded the Pope, each carrying a lighted candle as a symbol of the day's joy. As this magnificent procession entered the basilica, priests, religious and laymen began chanting the *Credo* in Latin. When the throne on which the Pope sat came into view, the traditional trumpets sounded the notes of the papal march which mingled with the Gregorian chant of the hymn of faith.

After the Pope had prayed and received the cardinals, he heard the three ceremonial petitions for the canonization of Martin de Porres. These were interspersed with further prayer by the Pope and the congregation. Then, after the choir had sung *Veni Creator Spiritus*, came the moment when the Pope, standing before his throne, uttered the words which elevated Martin de Porres to sainthood:

"In honor of the Holy Trinity, for the exaltation of the Catholic Faith and the spread of the Christian religion, by the authority of Our Lord Jesus Christ, of the holy apostles Peter and Paul and by our own authority: After mature deliberation and having implored divine assistance, with the favorable vote of Our venerable brothers, the Cardinals of the Holy Roman Church, the patriarchs, Archbishops and Bishops present in the city, we declare and define Blessed Martin de Porres, confessor, to be a saint and to be inscribed in the lists of the saints; establishing that his memory be duly commemorated among the holy confessors with pious devotion every year on the anniversary of his death, that is November 3. In the name of the Father and of the Son and of the Holy Ghost, Amen."

The bells of St. Peter's burst into joyous peals and the clear full tones of the organ resounded in triumphant swells of music. The son of Don Juan de Porres and Ana Velasquez was the newest saint to be inscribed on the rolls of the Holy Roman Catholic Church.

During the Offertory of the Mass which followed, the traditional ceremonial offerings of bread, wine, water, candles and doves in beautifully gilded cages were brought to the Pope. After Mass he returned to his portable throne and was carried out of the church as the thunderous cheers and applause of the crowd mingled with the hymns sung by the Sistine Choir. A triduum of prayer in honor of St. Martin was held at the ancient Dominican Church of Santa Maria sopra Minerva in Rome during the three days which followed his canonization.

His Eminence Francis Cardinal Spellman, Archbishop of New York, who was one of the thirty-eight princes of the Church attending the canonization rites, immediately radiogrammed Auxiliary Bishop John J. Maguire, Vicar-General of New York, that he had named the parish at Red Oaks Mill, Poughkeepsie, New York, for St. Martin de Porres on the day of the saint's canonization, the first parish in the New York archdiocese to be named for St. Martin.

On May 7, Pope John held a special audience for the thousands of pilgrims who had come from all over the world to witness Brother Martin's canonization. The audience was held in the Hall of Benedictions and some 5,000 pilgrims were present when the Pope referred to the three great loves of Martin's life: Christ crucified, Our Lady of the Rosary, and Saint Dominic. The Pope concluded his informal talk by saluting Martin as "the angel of Lima," recalling the saint's devotion to the sick and the poor of all classes. "May the light of his life illuminate for men the road of Christian social justice," the Pope implored, "and of universal charity without distinction of color or of race."

The Archbishop of Lima, Juan Cardinal Landazuri, expressed the thanks of the pilgrims. Various gifts were presented to the Pope, including a bronze copy of Father McGlynn's statue of St. Martin. The original statue was also in Rome at the time of the canonization and was a gift on behalf of the New York Province. Dominican Fathers Norbert Georges and Edward Hughes were present with Father McGlynn. A group of Italian barbers presented the Pope with a miniature set of barber's instruments. Several portable altars to be sent to the missions in honor of St. Martin were also presented.

On November 9, 1579, when Father Juan Antonio Palanco baptized a tiny brown baby called Martin, he had no idea that he had baptized a saint of the Holy Roman Catholic Church—St. Martin de Porres.

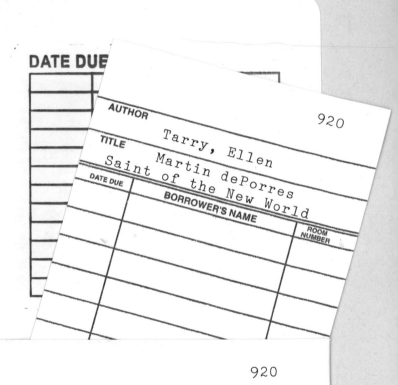

DATE DUE

AUTHOR		920
Tarry, Ellen		
TITLE Martin dePorres Saint of the New World		

DATE DUE	BORROWER'S NAME	ROOM NUMBER

920

Martin dePorres
Saint of the New World

Tarry, Ellen

DEMCO